Angels

Wallace and ... own

Contents

Foreword to the 2017 edition   5

The Red Sea Syndrome   9

'It's the Work I Want You to Do…'   15

Into a Strange Land   21

Angels on the Walls   27

Spiritual Regeneration   33

A Touch of God's Power   39

Learning to Take 'Faith Risks'   45

Barbed Wire and Wild Horses   53

The Coming of Titus   65

'The Tower is Falling Down…'   75

'They Empty the Bins on Mondays!'   83

Telephones, Taxis and Fire!   91

'He Sets Fire to Things, You Know'   99

'Tell the People… What Their Sins Are'   111

Wild Grapes   119

Timid Tabbies, Cute Kittens and Toffee-nosed Toms   125

Children Are People Too   131

Trouble Valley   139

The Helped Becoming the Helpers   147

Painting a 'Faith Picture'   153

Does God Speak Through Dreams?   159

'It's My Mother. She Keeps Coming to See Me'   165

The Joshua Strategy   173

'I've Got to Open up the Church!'   177

Sending Out the Workers   183

The Lord Your God is With You   191

Conclusion   197

Clipboard   203

Preface

Foreword to the 2017 edition

Charles Spurgeon famously wrote: 'I do not know how to explain it, but I believe angels have a great deal to do with the business of this world'.

The 'Angels on the Walls' Mary and I first perceived around our Birmingham vicarage and church in 1986 have dramatically and wonderfully touched our life for these last thirty years. Biblically, of course, that is the work of angels. Messengers of God. The telling forth of God's way forward.

We arrived in Birmingham with little or no clue of ministry in large suburban council estates. The local authority mostly owned my new parish, although 'right to buy' of the 1980 legislation was beginning to reveal significant appreciation of owning one's own house. To Mary and myself, together with our three children, Jeremy, Nicholas and Elizabeth, it was a new and quite shocking social environment. We found ourselves, on the very first day, surrounded by the sheer violence, viciousness and seeming inhumanity of the longstanding gang locally named the 'Quinton Mob'. For many years, we discovered our vicarage/church walls had been their headquarters from whence they went forth to wreak appalling and abusive mayhem. The wider community stood in fear or even denial of the sheer lawlessness of thirty-five or so members of the gang. The police, at that time, stated that they lacked the powers to deal adequately with the out of control children and young people.

There seemed no way forward, but that's when God intervened through His holy angels and amazingly put us on an entirely new track for ministry. 'Angels on the Walls' is an account of this supernatural happening and consequential learning it propagated within us, St Boniface Church and the wider church.

I write this new preface in the shadow of the dreadful happenings within the Grenfell Tower. It was, I understand, mostly the poor who perished in the inferno. These lofty blocks used to be named 'council housing', and now 'social housing'. Perhaps they should be re-named 'dwellings for the poor'. Over the years, God has created in my heart a passion and even a love for the folk who live in such tower blocks with their surrounding maisonettes and large estates. Call them 'council' or 'social' or whatever. In this book, I call them the 'hidden poor'.

Social housing, now and then, no longer presents the classic working class, storybook values such as 'salt of the earth'. At the beginning of our 'angelic' journey in Birmingham, many of the 'sink estates' were a raw wound in our society – rapidly becoming septic. However, in the midst, one met many, many folks with great traditional values often feeling incredulous at what was happening around them. Yet for most people, as myself in those early years, the deprivation within large suburban council estates remained hidden and often beyond professional empathy. Few professional people lived within the estates.

Nevertheless, in the midst of our three such estates, I have witnessed the extraordinary emergence of a vibrant intergenerational community church. It started, not with a proactive 'us', but within the leading and call of those 'holy angels' that God himself placed on our walls.

The original small, mostly elderly congregation had lost its faith dynamic, and been overwhelmed by the threatening social issues surrounding them. The drawbridge had been drawn up. Yet, under God's hand, the church family has grown and flourished to become His lighthouse to the one-time fractured community it serves. Moreover, as this fellowship in Christ bloomed, as it still blooms in 2017, so the neighbourhood has been powerfully and objectively transformed. Our strap-line of *the spiritual affects the physical* has proved true. Prayer coupled with complimentary action can regenerate communities. Over the years, as well as ongoing prayer, the renewed fellowship expended energy in championing physical regeneration as well as helping develop decent schools and an attractive urban environment. For example, the growth of a secular community choir and joined up children and youth work; together with ongoing development for leisure. It's all part of the gospel imperative. The church is about strengthening the poor, and not simply turning itself into a bourgeois religious enclave.

Over my eighteen years of toil, joy and tears in this 'outer' council estate church, I grew to value profoundly the often disempowered and 'poor' people of the area. I think they are great. Especially when they come to faith in Jesus Christ. We witnessed the shackles drop away with the emergence of spiritually transformed, fresh, authentic and vibrant characters who have much to teach the so-called middle classes. What you see is what you get! Often, we discovered, the folks lived on the feelings of the moment; and were astonishingly open, loving and giving. I've heard talk of 'hearts of gold', and while I abhor the lack of biblical understanding in such a phrase, I recognise the sentiment behind it. Buried beneath relative poverty, pain, abuse and broken relationships lie possibilities and potential that exceed all expectations.

'Angels on the Walls' exists to share the passion Mary and I feel for the 'hidden poor' of all eras. Many are poor in the sense of material wealth, some are reliant on often inadequate benefits, many are poor in the sense of formal education; many suffer disproportional broken relationships and abuse. But there is a richness of possibility in today's 'poor' areas. There is a richness of God's love to share with the many who feel outcast and 'done down' by society. Moreover, there is a richness of possibility to grow spiritually dynamic, culturally relevant, community churches.

If you are looking for a mission field, you need look no further than the 'poor' of our land. Here you will find the unchurched; from the base of council/social housing. During our time of ministry in the Birmingham estates, fewer than four adults and one child in a thousand attended their Anglican church, and few attended any other denomination. I strongly suspect nothing much has changed. In my conclusion of this book, I suggest – with a heavy heart: *'many council estate Anglican churches are reaching out with gnarled, aged arms of the post war culture into a society that venerates the new, the young and the self.*

Take heart, God is calling his people to come alongside the poor of our land. Within such ministry, you will find God given and God directed opportunity to grow committed all age fellowships of true Christian disciples. Here among the 'poor and needy', you will find God's heart. It is, I passionately believe, in God's heart to transform poverty into riches.

Come with me into this book as we explore the cultural values. We seek to break down churchy barriers, with our witness of the sheer power of God's Holy Spirit; and discover God's heart of love towards todays 'poor'. A love that is in no way limited by human class, sexuality, background or profession.

God's angelic presence still casts His supernatural overshadowing over all areas of human endeavour. However, the great need in our generation, it seems to me, is particularly stirring in our deprived areas. Amongst the poor.

What the Lord requires of His people is the devoted, Christ-centred few to pioneer the way.

How about you?

Wallace and Mary Brown, Herefordshire, Autumn 2017

1

The Red Sea Syndrome

Stretch out your hand over the sea to divide the water.

Exodus 14:16

The vicarage doorbell shrilled again. I looked at the warm cosy fire, the freshly prepared supper and groaned inwardly. After all, this was my night off and Mary and I were attempting to unwind and spend 'quality time' together. Outside it was a damp, chilly November evening and, as usual, there was a sense of foreboding in the very atmosphere. The large council estate that surrounded the vicarage emanated trouble, apathy, fear and especially violence. The normal noise of overloud radios, barking dogs, revving cars, shouted arguments and the occasional drunken roaming gang filled the air. Tonight, as always, the vicarage family felt isolated and vulnerable.

Earlier the same evening, I had reluctantly opened the front door to a 'needy traveller'. At least he said he was needy. Certainly he was in need of a wash and sobering up. He unravelled his complicated tale as I waited patiently for the punch line, which would be his dire need of money. I have a policy never to give money on the doorstep, but to give real care in other ways. However, the night was unpleasant and the story endless, so I'd coughed up a pound and a 'meaningful' smile. Suddenly my problem was gone. No doubt the 'local' had a further customer. More to the point, I could get back to my chair. I felt guilty, but warm. So when the doorbell rang again I answered it grudgingly, and a young man swayed forward out of the gloom. Although clean and tidy, vapid eyes and the aroma of alcohol made him appear somewhat strange. I felt vaguely uneasy. His hands were behind his back.

'How can I help?' I asked, without much enthusiasm.

In slurred monosyllables he managed to tell me simply, 'I don't know what to do.'

It was 9.30 p.m., raining and dark. I asked his name and then bowed to the inevitable.

'Come on in, John. Let's talk about it.' Seething inwardly, I led him into the study. On closing the door behind us, I turned to see John grasping a huge, shiny, sharp-looking butcher's knife, pointed in my direction. Its honed edge glinted under the 150-watt light bulb. I felt my breath getting shorter, my lungs seizing up. All sorts of thoughts suddenly surged through my mind. What an idiot I was, allowing this armed, drunken, disturbed, possibly drugged man over the threshold in the first place! And what about Mary and our children? Would he 'stick' me and then go on the rampage through the house?

What right had I to subject my family to the troubles of the area? The emotions flashed through me in a sort of slow motion, almost like a dream, yet the cold steel only a few feet away stamped an unequivocal reality.

I was helpless to know what to do. So I suggested inanely, 'Do you want to put your knife on the desk?'

John merely looked through me. His flat, empty eyes were slightly out of focus, with a menacing voidness. The knife remained very firmly clutched in his hand and I noticed his strained white knuckles. The situation was deteriorating. And I felt totally inadequate.

Then, to my amazement and consternation, and right in the midst of all my swirling emotions, a totally unforeseen supernatural understanding of Johns predicament came directly into my mind. It was almost like a voice saying, 'Wallace, this is what you must do.' I cannot explain why or how, but I knew God was there with me and speaking directly into the situation.

I turned to John, my mind still racing, and blurted out, 'John, your mother's a medium, isn't she? And some very strange things have gone on in your house, right back as far as you can remember. Isn't that right?'

No reaction.

My words continued to pour out: 'God is telling me about the dark spiritual power she has And how much it confuses you. How much you hate it. You even feel her influence all around you, in everything you do. Isn't that right? And you hate it. You don't really want it, do you?'

I sat down in astonishment. Was this really me saying these words to a knifeman? What if I'd got it all wrong? Such a dramatic word of knowledge was certainly not in my counselling handbook. Especially in this sort of dire situation.

For a moment he looked even more blank, and then gradually incredulous. 'How did you know that?' he whispered. 'I've never told anybody!' He slid down into the chair opposite me. The knife, I noticed, was now only loosely held across his knees.

I continued, 'John, there's more. God is much more powerful than the spirits your mother deals with. Believe me, he can really sort this out for you.'

He seemed to accept the idea. I started to pray in a way I'd never prayed before, and with my eyes wide open, watching him very carefully. Amazingly, John was quietly putting his knife down and I noticed that tears began to fill his eyes. The glazed, empty expression softened, and I felt myself turning towards him. I began to see yet another broken individual desperately in need of love, care and healing.

An hour later John left the vicarage. I've never seen him again, so I've no idea of the long-term effect. Anyway, perhaps that's God's problem rather than mine. At least John had glimpsed the reality of God.

As the door closed behind him, I almost ran back into the lounge. I was so hyped up by God speaking in such a dramatic way that I'd almost forgotten the sheer potential violence of the situation. I started to blurt out the story to Mary. Her expression closed up, and then she started to cry, tears rolling down her face.

'Isn't it enough to live in this awful place without people threatening to kill us?' she shouted in sobbing anguish. 'You bring my children to this estate and then you come in and tell me about a drugged man with a butcher's knife in my house! How do you expect me to react?'

'Never mind all that,' I declared, sounding like an arrogant thug myself. 'Won't you at least listen to what happened?'

She slammed the door on her way up to the bedroom, and I was left to reflect on my stupidity first, in allowing the man into. our house, and then not understanding the effect on Mary. Yet God had spoken. I felt stupid, confused, excited and hopeless... all at the same time. Later on, I tiptoed up to the bedroom and we both pretended to sleep.

Alienated from each other in an alien situation.

* * *

God had spoken suddenly and surprisingly one drab November night. In one millisecond he was at the root of John's problem while I was swanning around panicking and feeling generally helpless and hopeless. All my training and experience was of little use to me in that bizarre situation. Yet I witnessed him, as if in a dream, speaking into John's life swiftly, powerfully and accurately. It struck me with the force of a poleaxe. Why not expect God to speak dramatically and powerfully into everyday situations? Why not expect him to envision my programme of ministry? Why not expect him to be my 'boss', not in mere lip service but in stark reality? All I needed to do, or so it seemed in the simplicity of the moment, was to open my ears to him: to 'turn my radio on', as one Christian songwriter once suggested.

Moses himself must have known this truth. As he led the Hebrews out of Egypt towards the Promised Land, it became increasingly obvious that the re-established nation would be overtaken by the army of their oppressors. And then suddenly he was faced with the terrible barrier of the Red Sea stretching out before him. If Moses had been the average 'systemised' church leader, maybe he would have said to Aaron, 'Come on, let's organise a jumble sale so we can buy some boats.' Or perhaps he would have erected a fund-raising 'thermometer' to enhance donations from local industry in order to erect a bridge. What Moses did do was listen to God, hear what he said and then act in obedience to the command: 'Lift up your stick and hold it out over the sea. The water will divide.' *(Exodus 14:16, GNB)*

Later on, his protégé Joshua directed the nation to walk round the walls of Jericho seven times, just blowing their trumpets! The religious people of the time may well have suggested the alternative of forming a 'conquest committee' to formulate good ideas for taking the city. But Joshua took note of the God who speaks and acted in obedience, and the city was won. The people of God today are full of good ideas. Some of us vicars thrive on them! But what the church surely needs, and needs desperately, is 'God ideas' to bring about the opening of the sea, and the collapse of the walls, for the glory of God, as well as hard, obedient work *inspired* by God speaking into situations, dynamically and dramatically. Of course, hearing God is nothing new. Over all the centuries ordinary Christians have responded to God's dynamic voice. It's simply that God exploded in my mind the shocking concept that I'd been 'vicarised' and crowded into merely doing the job as it was presented to me; squeezed into an ecclesiastical system which, for all I knew, might bear more relation to Pharisaism than to serving the living God.

Religious duty and pious strategy can be a death sentence on ministries that start out in exciting faith. Funerals, baptisms, weddings, services, pastoral visits and church meetings had descended to the level of maintaining a system – and I knew, in my deepest heart, this raised all sorts of questions. Yet I also needed a system. I had studied my Bible well enough to know that our God is a God of order not chaos.

This is surely the paradox of ministry. The church needs to hear God and to work dynamically in his name, yet at the same time realise that the opening of the Red Sea doesn't happen every day. For instance, the Acts of the Apostles is a vibrant book of God's revelation, and at first glance we may think that's how the Christian life should be. Yet it was written over many years with most of the routine aspects missing. The whole of the New Testament displays the exciting joy of discerning God's calling, contrasted sharply with the straightforward hard work it propagates.

The truth of this perception was brought home to me one night in a dream. As I lay in bed I saw a pleasant English shoreline alongside a gently rolling sea. On the beach were many ministers digging furiously in the sand, not for recreation but with purpose. I went across and asked them what they were doing.

'Building a swimming pool, of course, so that people can swim,' was the sense of the answer.

'But why don't you swim in the sea?' I asked the toiling vicars.

They were too busy to listen. And the sand kept falling into their hole. Sadly I left them to their unending labour and went for a swim in the sea.

How hard many ministers work: toiling and sweating for the kingdom, intent and single-minded. The Lord seemed to say to me, 'So many don't know they have to listen and then do what I tell them. They work and work on their own agendas, often getting nowhere. Why don't they look up to heaven and listen to me?'

I sensed God was showing me how he longs to release his leaders and his church today. Release them from slavery to ecclesiastical systems and methods, that they may somehow bathe in the free, vast, mighty sea of his power. If only God's church, of whatever denomination or non-denomination, could grasp the Red Sea Syndrome of Moses!

This book is the result of a personal seeking to use 'God ideas' rather than simply good ideas to rebuild a church community. It's the true story of arriving as the new vicar of a run-down church in the middle of a massive council estate sprawling on the edge of Birmingham, full of good ideas and potential. And of finding, instead of instant success, a personal pit of utter despair where only the Lord could have 'lifted me out of the slimy pit... [and] set my feet on a rock' *(Psalm 40:2)*, where all my pre-packed notions of spirituality and schemes of mission were ground into the dust of helplessness and hopelessness. It's the story of discovering the Red Sea Syndrome, so that we could begin to perceive the riches of God's ideas and schemes rather than the poverty of man-made strategy, and then start to tackle the horrific problems that surrounded us, both on the estate and in the church, using *God's agenda*.

I will start at the beginning: Sheffield, England...

2

'It's the Work I Want You to Do...'

Your word is a lamp to my feet

Psalm 119:105

It was 2 a.m. and I jolted awake feeling cold, sweaty and full of terror. 'This is not how it should be,' I thought, because only a few short hours before, at 7.40 p.m. precisely, I'd committed my life to Jesus Christ.

It was shortly after my thirtieth birthday. Mary and I, with our three children, had settled down comfortably in a pleasant detached house on the outskirts of Sheffield. I was District Engineer with East Midlands Gas – a recent promotion with excellent prospects for the future. My commitment was a decision that had been haunting me for some time. Ever since my father had died with a brain tumour I'd felt unsettled in myself. 'Is this all there is to life? Am I merely to live a relatively few short years then... finished? Is there just the blackness and oblivion of total death?' The questions

haunted me. Yes, I was doing well in my chosen career, but was that enough? Was that the sum purpose of my life? Already I had fallen into the career trap of putting business in front of wife and family.

I somehow knew that God had been beckoning me; yet there is a great step between knowing and doing. A few years previously Neil Armstrong had said, 'One small step for man, one giant leap for mankind,' as he left the relative security of the lunar module *Eagle* and stepped onto the virgin face of the earth's moon. He saw clearly how one step could take him from safety into the unknown. I had to step into the spiritual unknown, and that was a hard decision of the will. Yet, having made certain no one was around, I sat and prayed, 'Lord Jesus, I'm not sure if you even exist, but if you do I invite you into my heart.'

As I prayed, I saw a picture in my mind's eye – an entirely new experience for me. The mind picture started as a huge ink blot that completely covered my inner vision. As I continued my prayer, from somewhere inside I felt a new conviction that God was God. Simultaneously the ink spot slowly withdrew and took shape, depicting the form of a menacing spider. Gradually it became the merest speck, then disappeared completely.

Two years later, as I related this experience to the then Bishop of Leicester, he remarked, 'Ah well, you know what that was: it was the "old enemy" retreating from your life.'

It made sense as a spiritual representation of what was happening to me: as I gave Jesus Christ authority to be my Lord, so Satan withdrew. He had no other choice because the power and presence of Christ overwhelms evil. It was an experience that was to be of great significance to me. Indeed, it's clear from the Bible that God is a speaking God. Pictures, dreams and 'words' are all ways God speaks his mind to his church: always, of course, in accordance with Scripture.

In bed that same evening, I'd prayed, 'Lord, keep me safe this night.' Paradoxically, I entered a maelstrom of activity. I was safe, but within myself I experienced the conflict raging over me in the spiritual realms. I began, even then, to understand that the Christian faith is no walkover. Jesus Christ said, 'Take up your cross and follow me'... and surely he meant into the battlefield of the world, the flesh and the devil.

Over the next few months, my thoughts became dominated by the alien concept of becoming an ordained minister in the Church of England. Denomination was not an issue, but I believed God was saying, 'Wallace, I want you to become a vicar in the Anglican church.' Mary, a recent convert herself, was really pleased, and the children were excited by the idea of an adventure.

* * *

'The bishop will see you now,' said the secretary at Bishop's Lodge in Leicester, some five years later. Even though I'd been through the

Anglican system of selection conference and theological college, I was like a schoolboy summoned by the headmaster regarding some minor misdemeanour. I felt out of my depth in the traditional 'establishment' of the church. Almost an interloper.

Even the waiting-room was another world. Edwardian bookcases lined the walls, full of profound-looking theological volumes; an exquisitely patterned Persian carpet lay underfoot; up-market magazines were carefully scattered on the beautifully polished oak table. Outside, the gardener toiled on the finely cut lawn amid gorgeous colours of autumn shrubs.

I walked nervously into the bishop's study. 'Well, I suppose you want me to fix you up with a title,' said the old gentleman. He seemed just as nice as when we had talked about that 'spider' some years previously. And what did he mean by a title? Was I to become Sir Wallace, or had he already recognised some deep and previously unseen quality in me to become a 'Lord Bishop' of the future? It turned out that 'title' was an ecclesiastical term for a curate's first job. And yes, I did want him to 'fix me up'.

A few hours later, I arrived at Oadby Rectory. The door opened and John Tonkin cheerfully asked me my business. I was to learn over the next six years that John is a wonderfully positive man of God, always looking for the best in people and often finding it. He was just right to be my training vicar – a perfect foil for my natural cynicism and tendency to mood swings. I falteringly explained. Clearly the bishop had forgotten to telephone, so here I was, once again, feeling foolish and inadequate.

Over the following years, those feelings of inadequacy were supplanted by the beguiling flavour of success. Mary and I started weekly services in a local high school and spearheaded the building of a new church plant called St Paul's. The young, professional and growing congregation was spiritually active and generally thriving. With the building complete and finances in order, I felt ready for anything.

How proud I became. Flushed with the power of coming from an unchurched background and yet leading a flourishing young congregation, success merely blinded my eyes and ears, and I became convinced that I was somehow God's gift to a messed-up church. It was simply a matter of 'being spiritual', offering relevant worship, engaging with issues of the moment and being young and vital. And anyway, didn't success breed success?

When my five-year contract was up it was time to move on. Little did I know that this would herald the beginning of a deep personal darkness: a 'dark night of the soul'. It was pre-empted by a word from God to Mary which simply stated, 'The work into which I am calling you is not easy. There will be times of great difficulty. There will be times when all you will be able to do is fall at my feet and ask for my help, but I will be with you. It is the work to which I have called you, and you will know this. You will know that I am with you. It is the work I want you to do. Many people will be saved through your obedience.'

Yet it all began so easily. I was invited to apply for the position of Vicar at a 'renewed inner-city church'. God had spoken through Scripture and even through a church meeting that this was just the right place for us. And the following Monday we drove over to Birmingham to view the church from the outside and quietly pray.

'Come and Worship the Living God!' read a massive sign on the church gable end. Just right! And what a change from the 'thermometers of faithlessness' that adorn the public presentation of so many churches.

As we looked at the vicarage, Mary commented breathlessly, 'It's exactly like the one I saw in a dream the other night.' The evidence for God's call to this place became absolute in our minds. Through a further series of apparent coincidences and assurances from our daily Bible reading scheme, we concluded that this church was exactly God's plan for us.

Then the letter arrived: 'I regret to inform you…' We were absolutely stunned: Mary almost fainted with shock, and I broke down and wept. It seemed to me that the whole of my Christian life had collapsed… my faith was surely all built on sand. Doubt and unbelief reached round me like a dark cloak, and pummelled all my perceptions. 'It's all nothing,' I decided. 'God has no interest in me!'

Even time seemed to be affected, and everything went into slow motion. Our wonderful experience of God speaking and leading was utterly ravaged. And yet it had been so real. There was no sense in it. The heavens became as brass, and we felt totally abandoned and lost.

I still know God was leading us. Was it a deliberate and necessary teaching process, or was his plan somehow thwarted? Is it possible for God's ways to be changed by mere mortal man? I was tempted to ask, 'Does God lead his people merely to fall?'

How can we understand such deep things? The pain lingers even now, not because we especially wanted to go to that particular place, but because it really had been a matter of faith. God, I felt, had let us down. Which way could I turn? We had not yet learned to have faith in God himself, rather than faith in our own faith.

* * *

I didn't like Birmingham. At least I didn't like the impression I had of the place from the mid 60s when I was courting Mary. I was utterly engrossed in her, but her home city was a definite turn off. Concrete, concrete and yet more concrete filled my memory. But strangely, even in the midst of my sense of abandonment, God would not let Birmingham out of my mind. Funny how you can have a burden for a place you don't naturally like, but that's how it was. A mere two weeks after 'the letter', out of the blue a letter arrived from the Bishop of Birmingham, inviting me to look at St Boniface Church.

As I drove round the area, I realised with a shock that I'd never even considered ministry in the outer council estates. In my limited thinking, the inner city had all the excitement, the leafy suburbs all the possibilities, the country was too comfortable and sleepy, but the council estates… well, they were just impossible! Yet here I was being offered a new ministry right in the centre of three massive outer council estates. And the vicarage was a sort of large council house right next door to the church! What would Mary say?

However, there have been few moments in my life when I have known God so completely in charge of events, and my interview with Bishop Hugh Montefiore was one such time. The Spirit of the Lord was upon us and I knew from that moment he was calling me to St B's. It was not the usual level of faith, but a certainty in my heart: impossible to express because it is a matter of the soul. In double-fast time the church was offered and I accepted.

3

Into a Strange Land

How shall we sing the Lord's song in a strange land?

Psalm 137:4 (AV)

The vicarage was a mess: wallpaper hung off the walls; a ceiling had come down; water streamed into the dining room; pelmets and curtain rails lay in a jumbled heap outside the back door; windows were painted shut; smashed fences and a wrecked shed evidenced the work of vandals in and around the back garden. The grass had not been cut for well over a year and was matted and folded back on itself. Blackberry brambles freely twisted themselves around much of the luxuriant vegetation, while cultivated plants ran to seed or lay broken and trampled. It was like a jungle. We had to smile when we remembered the scripture God had revealed to us several months beforehand: 'If you can't even stand up in open country, how will you manage in the jungle?' (*Jeremiah 12:5, GNB*) The bottom of the jungle had become a local rubbish dump, complete with extremely smelly nappies.

We soon learned of the four burglaries suffered by the previous vicar during his final year. And even more telling, of the intruders who'd broken into the study, smeared excrement round the walls and then connected the garden hosepipe to soak the room and contents.

The church complex itself reflected the 60s open-plan style, so the vicarage and church lawns were inseparable. The reality of the area hit us hard as we heard about the rape of a child on the lawned area. We felt fearful for our 13-year-old daughter. On those same lawns, a gang roamed, lounging around the boundary walls and, as the weather turned from winter to spring, encroaching onto the Vicarage side, enjoying blatant sex, blaspheming, swearing and shouting in a drunkenly offensive manner. If we went outside at certain times, we had to run the gauntlet of offensive and crude remarks, as well as the threat of physical violence. My wife became fearful of going out. My children coped with the situation, but found life a feat of endurance. We had arrived in our council estate parish, and we felt like prisoners in a completely alien land.

Turning from the immediate church area to the parish itself, some of the social problems that occurred during the first few months included a double murder in a house just yards from the vicarage, when a man killed his wife and the visiting social worker; a policeman knifed outside the local pub, apparently without motive; an 86-year-old woman, housebound, deaf and partially sighted, raped in her own bed, her house a mere hundred yards from our back door; a police dog wounded with a machete as the police broke into a maisonette; a young man found hanged; a man armed with a blunt knife committing suicide in front of his five children; an elderly woman in permanent shock because children leered in at her while shouting and writing obscenities on her bedroom window; a security system installed in a local primary school for the safety of the teachers, a number of whom had been assaulted by parents, and who lived in fear of violence.

Adjoining the estate is a country park called the Woodgate Valley. We noticed that it was advertised as a place for bird-watching, walking and natural beauty. At first glance it was, and is, a beautiful area. Yet for us in those first months, the Valley became a symbol of much that was wrong with the neighbourhood. Two local gangs met and fought amid the discarded supermarket trolleys that littered the beautiful brook. The pleasant bridges were defaced by graffiti, and broken glass, litter and trash abounded on the carefully constructed pathways. A burned-out car adorned the bushes where the birds attempted to sing. Many years later, the growing church was able to tackle this dire situation, but for the moment we felt helpless.

The police were helpful, but had no answer other than to arrest when possible. Often, it seemed to me, the courts had little option other than to let the offenders go, and the same kids were back the next day, laughing at authority. Mounted police were seen in the Valley and a police helicopter often hovered overhead, but the trouble seemed only to get worse. I was told about one lad who, after being tied to a lamp post, was tortured with burning cigarette ends and physical brutality. I met one of the perpetrators some years later, and it appeared to mean nothing to him.

In the midst of this trauma, the church continued its traditional role. It appeared to be quite separate from what was happening in the locality – indeed some longstanding church members thought it was a congenial area apart from that estate. Barbed wire was fixed along the back of the church boundary to try and prevent destructive vandalism, but all it succeeded in doing was separating off the church from the community. Inside the church the small, established congregation engendered a club atmosphere. They were the remnant of an older 'respectable' working-class tradition who were determined to keep up standards. In reality, they had become a power group.

'How do you like it here?' Mary and I were continually asked. 'Are you settling down OK?'

'Yes,' I replied, tongue in cheek. And then would add truthfully, 'I really believe this is where God has called us.'

But in reality we were in a state of shock over problems around the vicarage, and of disgust about the happenings within the neighbourhood. The church, in the centre, appeared to have little reality. Was this all that Jesus Christ had to offer to the poor and needy? Or had God's people somehow missed the point? I noticed during Sunday worship that if I mentioned the name of Jesus, except within the liturgy, some people looked really embarrassed. It was all right to preach theological sermons from the pulpit, but to come down to the floor and just share with people about Jesus was almost too much. I felt alien and rejected within the church. I had the sense that if our church were 'congregational' rather than 'episcopalian', I would have been voted out on the grounds of 'too much about Jesus, not enough religion'.

Mary's diary from these early months reads: 'I feel totally alone: there is no help within the church and no help from the wider church. There is no refuge but God, and he seems very distant. I now know what it means to "fall at his feet and ask for his help", just as he told me even a year before we moved here.'

She was right. It was as if we had been plunged into a situation beyond our human resources and left to flounder. Nobody from the diocese asked the simple question, 'How's it going?' And because of the archaic religious system, there was absolutely no accountability. Not even a simple monthly report to a line manager. Nothing. Just a self-motivated sense of responsibility towards God himself.

I associated passionately with the psalmist who said, 'Save me, O God, for the waters have come up to my neck. I sink in the miry depths, where there is no foothold.' *(Psalm 69: 1-2)* That is exactly how I felt. It wasn't until some time afterwards that I realised God was painting a picture in my inner being of the dire needs of such areas, so that I could profoundly sense his yearning towards the poor and needy, and consequently have a powerful burden deep within for the forgotten council estates of our land. I believe that God was creating in my soul his passion for light to overcome darkness.

I remembered the words uttered by the Bishop of Birmingham as he sent me to St Boniface. He told me that things had been difficult in the church, but not why. He told me to go in and change things, but not how. He said, I don't mind whether I put in an Anglo-Catholic or an Evangelical. But I want someone who knows what he believes.' At my induction service Bishop Montefiore stated, 'I've given you a new vicar, and I'm expecting things to change. I'm also expecting you to work with him to develop the mission of this church…'

Because of the bishop's support and my personal calling from God, I knew I had the authority to lead the church forward, but how was I to go about it? I felt lonely, overwhelmed and depressed. I didn't sense the close presence of God in my increasingly weak prayer life, but I knew in my heart that God had a work for Mary and me. The question I kept asking myself was: HOW? HOW? HOW? I felt the desolation the Israelites in Babylon must have felt during the exile, when the psalmist said 'How shall we sing the Lord's song in a strange land?' *(Psalm 137:4, AV)*

* * *

On reflection, it was a very 'strange land' we had arrived in, first of all from my own personal point of view, developed from a life and ministry worked out in professional middle-class surroundings, but mainly because of a marked shift in the sociological patterns of outer estates. In the 50s and 60s the outer estates were rightly seen as working class. Most of the people had a 'salt of the earth' ethic, which although not specifically Christian related well to the timeless absolutes of the Christian faith.

Two examples from recent years show the immense change in sociological patterns. In 1995 the Church Times reported on the problems in one outer estate:

> A new church near Barnsley has spent £25,000 fortifying itself against its own community. Every entrance in St Andrews, on the crime-ridden estate of Kendray, is alarmed. There are sensors on the roof and around the building, and the windows are armour plated. Side gates are topped with spikes... 'We wanted the church to be the only building in the community that said "Welcome"... but we've had to admit defeat.'

I spoke personally to one of the ministers at St Andrew's. He told me the media articles were overblown, but rightly presented a terrible truth about this outer estate.

A second example is the Marsh Farm Estate in Luton. In the mid 1990s the national newspapers reported street riots as children and young people ran amok through the estate, burning and destroying. The area is mainly 1970s good quality council housing with some high-rise flats. There are tree-lined roads, a youth club building, community centre, shops and even a church. The whole area is reasonably well appointed with plenty of green open spaces. A recent report from the Joseph Rowntree Foundation tells us:

12 of the 13 [riots and violent disturbances of 1991/2] took place in council estates, most of which were large. All were low-income areas with long-standing social problems. All bar one comprised largely traditional houses with gardens. *(Anne Power and Rebecca Tunstall, Joseph Rowntree Foundation)*

One of many examples of outer-estate problems in Birmingham itself comes from a fairly modern estate church in the eastern suburbs, which was 'fire bombed' with a stolen car. Joy-riders backed up as near as possible to the church doors and set the car alight. The resultant fireball smashed into the church and along the internal corridor towards the vicarage. Only the noise and resulting tumult saved the vicarage family. In Birmingham, the last four major church fires have been in outer estates.

Of course, at the time of my arrival in my outer-estate parish, I had no idea of such things. They were not on the public or church agenda! I merely felt a gigantic sense of isolation, which rapidly grew into overwhelming failure. Illogically, I began to believe I was the problem. I had no idea that all over the UK ministers of all denominations, who worked in such areas, were suffering equal difficulties.

In the midst of this new-found isolation and confusion of mind and spirit, Mary and I continued to call out to the Lord. But it seemed only to get worse…

4

Angels on the Walls

'We prayed to our God and posted a guard day and night to meet this threat.'

Nehemiah 4:9

Elizabeth arrived home in tears. 'They're on the walls again,' she sobbed. My heart sank as I heaved myself up to make for the front-room window. Mary reached out and drew her daughter tightly to her, distress etched on both their faces.

'Don't you care? Look at what all this is doing to us!' she accused. Desperation emanated from every word. 'I can't stand any more of this. Why don't we just pack up and go somewhere else, where people are nice?'

At the window I saw the usual scene. Gang members were lolling around the walls, shouting and swearing. A bottle crashed to the ground and shattered on our front path. Others were intent on the notice board, ripping off the latest offering and defacing the painted sign with a knife. In the morning I knew I would find discarded contraceptives. My heart fluttered as I considered, once again, what to do. If I called the police, the youngsters would just sidle away to return after a few hours, in triumph. If I went down to them, any comment would produce a gale of aggressive laughter followed by insulting remarks. I had no answer.

'Oh, it's just the Quinton Mob,' commented one church member in an offhand manner. 'They've been around here for ages. At least seven years.' He dismissed our devastation in a mere few words, as if it were nothing. After all, he didn't have to face crude and intimidating behaviour each time he went out of his front gate.

'Last vicar was a boxing champion, you know. He used to sort them out.' The obvious implication was that I had failed to deal with them. It was my fault. 'Ran after them, he did,' he added in afterthought.

'Didn't do him much good,' I muttered darkly to myself on the way home. 'All those burglaries
and the vandalism of the study. There has to be a better way.'

The following evening, I peered surreptitiously out of the bedroom window. There were about 35 of them, mostly older teenagers. The continuous, noisy, scornful banter was punctuated by long swigs from beer bottles. I remembered the often-told story of how, a few years previously, they had destructively closed down a neighbouring church youth club. My shoulders sagged as I went downstairs and flopped in front of the television.

'Wallace, what are we going to do?' Mary's voice pleaded.

Angrily I shrugged and turned away.

'My heart's palpitating again,' she commented mournfully. 'We can't go on like this, can we?'

I shrank deeper into the armchair.

'And the church hall windows will be broken again in the morning. It'll be the house next. Don't you care?'

It was too much. I threw myself out of the chair and stormed into the kitchen. The door received a very sharp kick on the way. I heard Mary following me, and felt cornered in my own despair; trapped by total frustration and the inability to deal with the overwhelming situation.

The following Sunday morning I came back from church even more depressed. The congregation numbers were continuing to decrease – the first time in my life such a thing had happened. And after the service someone had scornfully remarked, 'How long have you been here now?' I had smiled pastorally instead of 'biffing' him.

* * *

It was two o'clock in the morning when God spoke his dramatic word to Mary. She had been spreadeagled over the lounge floor (she told me later), wailing and beseeching God for a way forward through our immense difficulties. Tearfully and angrily she stormed the very gates of heaven.

Totally unexpectedly her thoughts were directed to the book of Nehemiah. And with a flash of insight she suddenly understood our problem and saw it all from an entirely different perspective. She excitedly dashed upstairs to waken me: 'Come on, Wallace, get up! God has been speaking to me. I've got to tell you about it. You see, it's all in Nehemiah!'

I stirred and grunted in protest.

'The problem with the gang round the walls here – it's not just a physical thing. It's like Satan has a grip on what's happening on the physical level from *his* spiritual plane. Do you see? He's the darkness! He's the problem! Wallace, the kids round the walls – we have to fight it on a spiritual level to break the hold.'

She looked grandly enthusiastic. Just like the Mary of old. 'God just told me to read Nehemiah, and I did. It's amazing. You read it and see.' Her voice lifted eagerly.

The story of Nehemiah is truly quite extraordinary. He was the Hebrew cupbearer to the Babylonian king, Artaxerxes, during the time of the exile after the fall of Jerusalem in 587 BC. After a time of seeking God through weeping, mourning and fasting, Nehemiah spoke to the king and requested, 'Send me to [Jerusalem] where my fathers are buried so that I can rebuild it.' (*Nehemiah 2:4*) Of course, when he arrived, the walls of the city had been torn down. Furthermore, groups of raiding parties under the neighbouring war-lord Sanballat were constantly attacking the walls of Jerusalem, hoping to gain control of the Judaean territory.

'Imagine taking that step of faith,' said Mary. 'Going back to Jerusalem to reconstruct the city and then finding all those people against him. Not just Sanballat's lot, but also the inhabitants. He must have been so despondent.'

Having grudgingly resigned myself to this middle-of-the-night talk, I replied, 'But look, God told him to do it, so he always was going to provide a way. Nehemiah just had to find it.'

'But don't you see, Wallace? It's the same sort of problem as we have.' Her eyes opened wide. 'And he must have felt just as hopeless as we do, because Sanballat and his lot were much more hostile than our pathetic teenagers. And look, it even talks about *walls!*'

Mary couldn't contain her enthusiasm as she added excitedly, 'Look what Nehemiah says: "So we rebuilt the wall... we prayed to our God and posted a guard day and night to meet this threat." *(Nehemiah 4:6,9)* We've got the same needs. Obviously not as dramatic, but equally as real. God has called us to build up his church at Quinton, but his work is being frustrated. Wallace...' her voice rose to a crescendo, 'we've just got to pray and put guards on the walls. The same as they did.'

'Come on, Mary,' I answered derisively. 'How can we place guards?' And then I added sarcastically, 'What do you want me to organise? The SAS or maybe a church vigilante group?'

She sank down in a helpless heap.

The following morning I lay in a hot bath thinking over my hurtful ridicule and discovered I was inwardly impressed by Mary's ideas. Nehemiah had come to a broken-down city. Vandals were threatening to overrun the walls and take the city. God's work was in danger of being wiped out even before it started. There were definitely parallels.

I went downstairs for breakfast. 'Go on then – what does the Lord say about our situation through Nehemiah? I asked self-consciously.

Mary accepted my unspoken apology and said, 'Let's wait on God and see.' She recorded the answer in her diary: 'We asked God how we could put guards on our walls. He gave us the understanding to place guardian angels there. We were to do this each day. And to continue to pray, just like Nehemiah.'

The very next day, Mary and I went out and prayed 'on location'. Feeling slightly foolish, I asked God to place guardian angels all round the walls, to make them safe, and to bring godliness to our lawns and boundaries. It felt good.

The effect was immediate and astonishing. Within a few days the gang started to break up. From the 35 swearing, screaming youths of the previous week, the number dropped to about ten and then by the following week to a mere two or three. Mary and I continued to go out and pray day by day: 'Lord, keep your guardian angels round these walls, please.'

And so he did. The relief was absolute. After year upon year of human failure, the terrible 'siege' of church and vicarage was broken by the supernatural holy presence of God's angels. People started to come in unhindered. My family unexpectedly tasted freedom, and it was wonderful. Mary was able to walk out of the house, and I could relax. What was more, the Quinton Mob did not move to pastures new – they totally broke up! Those years of belligerent menace simply ended with one stroke of God's mighty hand.

∗ ∗ ∗

So it was that Mary and I started to understand the supremely important principle that *the spiritual affects the physical*. During those six months of terror, we had perceived merely the physical problem. We hadn't understood the much more sinister spiritual battle over the church. The Quinton Mob and the 'enemy', in some sort of unholy alliance, had almost succeeded in the devastation of spiritual life. Any sense of local community was virtually non-existent, the church was almost faithless, and I wondered if the previous vicarage family had become victims, as I later learned of divorce and the vicar leaving the ministry.

Over subsequent years, teams of intercessors have continued to pray around the church as new generations of children come of age, and small groups choose the church walls as their meeting place. Each new situation has to be tackled afresh. We still pray for 'angels on the walls'. Why? Because the battle is ongoing; the narrow path never ceases to be narrow and this world always tends back to sin rather than holiness.

As I have visited other outer-estate churches, I have become aware of unperceived battles. The clergy work so hard at being excellent pastors, and deeply care for church and community, yet I wonder if many miss, like I did, the profound spiritual reality that surrounds every work of God. As C. S. Lewis asserts with his remarkable perception: 'They claim to see fern seed and can't see an elephant ten yards away in broad daylight.' The everyday detail of tangible facts tends to so overwhelm us that we find difficulty in perceiving the broader picture of the profound conflict going on all around us on the spiritual plane. Yet St Paul clearly states, 'Our struggle is not against flesh and blood, but against the rulers, against the authorities, against the powers of this dark world and against the spiritual forces of evil in the heavenly realms. *(Ephesians 6:12)* The spiritual consequence is an anarchy of demonic power, which leads to the growing lawlessness within the outer estates that we so clearly witness today.

However, awareness of the spiritual battle means the beginning of regeneration and certainly not the end, as we were shortly to discover for ourselves...

5

Spiritual Regeneration

'You are the light of the world.'

Matthew 5:14

The frowning man looked at his watch, slowly and pointedly, his eyes regarding me in a scornful, calculating way. It's amazing that right in the middle of a sermon a part of your mind can stray even as the words come out of your mouth. And my mind settled firmly on Mr Catchpole. Others in the dwindling congregation were reacting in different ways. One or two had that glazed expression, and even had I started talking about 'lust in the life of the Anglican vicar', their countenance would not have changed one iota. Some did not like the (to them) new gospel teaching: incomprehensible religious theology was preferable – it was less threatening. A small group of ladies were whispering to one another. Was it a theological worry they were discussing, or had I forgotten to remove some toothpaste from my chin? Amazingly, a few people actually looked interested and even excited. But Mr Catchpole had firmly captured my thoughts and I could feel the confidence draining out of me as I stood in the lonely pulpit. What was he thinking? And was it true?

Mary was also sitting in the congregation. She was not enjoying herself. She felt alienated and rejected. At least I had a clear job to do, and the authority that goes with it. Mary was confined in the Vicarage because of the difficulties surrounding our home, and in the church she was a captive of expectations and hinted comments. She also had to cope with a distraught and darkly brooding husband. Mary spent many hours in our bedroom crying, homesick for the friends and Jesus-centred Christians left behind. Her personal ministry of prophetic insight, teaching and leadership support, which had developed so clearly in our previous situation, now lay in tatters. Would she ever be used in these capacities again? It appeared, in the pain of the moment, that there were no future possibilities. She would say to me, 'It's all right for you. At least you've got a proper position and job. I don't know what my role is at all. I just feel lost. Don't you see?'

Of course life had become progressively difficult for the folk at St B's over the past few years. The congregation had always been 'respectable', with a good working-class ethic. Many of them came from private semis on the edges of the parish, with a sprinkling of people from the older council estate. But the building of massive new estates on the doorstep had totally changed the social structures of the area. These respectable older folk had become increasingly alienated within the new community, and were experiencing a growing sense of powerlessness in the face of a culture they didn't understand. Within the church, they wished to preserve 'values', which equated in their minds with traditional Anglicanism. They were becoming powerless in the community and yet more and more vociferous within the church. It was to be a bastion of what was 'right'. And so the power group came into being. In their mind they were saving the church for posterity; in reality they were building barriers against a new culture. Mr Catchpole was the guru of the group, and the new vicar was, perhaps, the adversary.

We have since discovered that most outer-estate churches are 'ruled' by otherwise disempowered older people: the remnant of the old 'working class', who are completely at odds with the society in which they live, retreating to the church with their backs against the wall. They enjoy the relative safety of their church and are scared of opening the door to the 'riff raff out there', terrified of losing what little they have.

Often clergy will overtly pander to power groups. On the one hand it is obvious that such groups stop the life of the church swelling, and yet there is a genuine fear of losing most of their little congregation. If the minister does battle, there will soon be letters flying to the bishop and/or the group will just leave. So fear of failure always looms. In the outer estates, there seems little confidence in the Lord of the church 'restocking' the pews.

At St Boniface Church, in those early days of our ministry, the monetary subscription to the diocese had not been paid in full for some years, a major loan was outstanding, and the stewardship programme was poorly supported – all reflecting the banal level of spirituality. Consequently, the finances were in chaos.

I remember the treasurer being very excited because the collection at my induction was about £56.00. 'That's amazing,' he said. 'It's far more than we normally get.'

Mary and I were painfully aware that most of the money had come from the visiting folk of my old parish. They had overwhelmed the existing congregation in both vitality and numbers No, things had certainly not been easy at St B's over the past years.

Many in the church were feeling unsettled and even angry at the change in emphasis. I had taken the first step towards disbanding the choir by 'de-robing' it within my first week.

Not simply because it consisted of about six chattering, giggly teenagers who sat chewing gum and reading teenage magazines while 'singing' for their 50p wages, alongside an aged lady who didn't quite know what was going on. More importantly, they gave no sense of true worship or even involvement with God. The style of liturgy was also undergoing radical change, as I 'presented' the service rather than just reading the book.

But it was really the preaching that many found offensive. Week in and week out I proclaimed that Jesus is Lord and the need to be born again. I suspect Mr Catchpole felt more insulted by the gospel than my personal idiosyncrasies. Some came to the newly formed Lent course. They soon learned it was merely the same message dressed up in a different way. I was absolutely determined to have either a church where Jesus Christ was glorified or no church at all. On Sundays, after the service, I usually fell into a dark depression. Even our customary walk in the local National Trust area saw me despondently kicking the offending grass tufts: imagining Mr Catchpole's head, perhaps!

The situation looked bleak. Though God had moved supernaturally against the gang on the walls, the problems were overwhelming and inside the church there was only a glimmer of light. It seemed the devil had triumphed and we were to be led out in his victory parade.

* * *

That glimmer of light stemmed from the results of our first Lent course. Maureen Stand, who later showed herself to be a capable, loyal and generous person, had decided to give St B's another go. She dramatically came through to a renewed personal faith. Others rediscovered a faith that had grown cold. So we established a small group, meeting in the vicarage lounge, which was to become a prayer and fellowship base: a place to re-establish the spiritual 'candlestick' of the church. My constant preaching of the gospel had revealed that many of our existing congregation had little knowledge of the person of Jesus Christ. So there was no future in seeking to move the congregation on to new things until a right spiritual base had been established.

Snippets from those early traumatic-yet-exciting days stand out in my mind. For instance, the moment when our small group caught the vision of what the church must become in order to serve the area for the Lord.

Maureen reacted first. Her bubbly personality claimed attention as she theatrically shot forward in her chair. 'Do you know what I was reading this morning?' She paused for effect as we waited patiently for the answer to her rhetorical question, a smile beginning to play round her lips. Then she turned to Matthew's Gospel and read aloud: 'You are the light of the world. A city on a hill cannot be hidden... In the same way, let your light shine before men.' *(Matthew 5:14,16)*

'Do you see?' she insisted forcefully. 'It fits in so well with what we've just been talking and thinking about.' The other members nodded their agreement.

I'd been teaching the group about the way godlessness was so rife over the estate. In one area of the parish with a population of 3,000, I'd been dismayed to find that there were very few churchgoers of any denomination. This particular estate was wild and dangerous: gangs abounded, children swore at passers-by and prostitutes stood on some street corners. The local primary school was beset by violence and was one of the first in Birmingham to have a security system.

Nobody from that area came to St B's.

Such godlessness can often allow dark spiritual forces to dominate. So little change could be expected socially until the light of Christ could be shone from the church. It was as if spiritual forces 'hooked on' to problems surrounding our estates, as they do to an extent right across society. What we needed was for our church to 'pray Christ in' right across our patch – and to do that the church itself needed to become a focus of his light: spiritually regenerated and proclaiming the gospel. Leaders must recognise that this need is paramount for all churches.

Professor Christie Davies of Reading University has recently stated: 'The absence of religion leads to misconduct, crime and social disintegration,' and goes on to say, 'If you wanted to know whether crime was rising or falling... the graph of church attendance would be enough to tell you.' *(Daily Telegraph, 3rd Feb 1995)* In other words, godliness leads to lawfulness. Of course, churches have always known and understood this truth, but we have lost confidence in our own proclamation!

The church can be the biggest influence for restoration on the council estates. We can achieve this through Christ, even where money, social structures and community plans have proved themselves to be impotent. Spiritually, the local parish church can become a power house for restoration: we have the calling to destroy the dark spiritual forces that hold so many of our lost sheep in bondage.

We started to pray that God would restore the 'candlestick' of his presence to St B's by breaking down false power groups, renewing worship, and blessing the gospel preaching. Our objective was clear: with God's guidance, a strong, vibrant church could be built to shine his glorious light over and into the community, so that men, women and children might be saved.

* * *

'Don't expect me to darken the doors of this place again!' exploded Mr Catchpole as he hurriedly brushed past me at the end of the service a few weeks later. I saw his wife follow grim-faced behind, and then watched their car shoot off at an alarming pace.

The catalyst had been Remembrance Sunday. Although I personally have great respect for the sentiments expressed, and am a regular visitor to the British Legion, I had decided, prayerfully, not to stop the communion at exactly 11 a.m. for the two-minute silence, but instead to do so at a less obtrusive moment. However, my action seemed somehow to encapsulate everything that the Mr Catchpole power group stood against. And it was just the last straw. One member interrupted the worship, and another stormed out. Things had come to a head.

It was a straightforward confrontation of power. It could have been over any issue. And it was at that moment the power group disintegrated. Our prayers had brought about a new spiritual horizon, unseeable even a few weeks beforehand. The battle, we understood even more clearly, is a spiritual one... with physical manifestations. From that moment of sheer confrontation, the church gained a new sense of togetherness and purposefulness. Sometimes, leaders have to confront and destroy.

Over the next days and weeks I felt dreadful – in no way victorious. And the church attendance numbers continued on their downward track. Was I right? Had I personally ruined some of the older people's walk with God? Was God really in this? Or was I merely another megalomaniac vicar, destroying rather than building?

6

A Touch of God's Power

The fire will test the quality of each man's work.

1 Corinthians 3:13

'Come, Lord Jesus, bless Maureen with your Holy Spirit; immerse her in your presence; heal her with your love.'

During the second year of our ministry at Quinton, a few (fool)hardy souls sat around the vicarage front room wondering what would happen next. For several weeks we had been teaching our Tuesday Praise and Prayer group about God the Holy Spirit and proclaiming his transforming power. Now was the time for the big test. Would he really come?

I invited some group members to pray with me over Maureen, and as we placed our hands on her head she started to sway backwards and forwards, very gently at first. Then suddenly she toppled and lay prone on the carpet. The folk in the room looked on, some obviously troubled, some amazed and others incredulous. 'What on earth is going on?' – you could almost hear the unspoken question.

'What do we do now?' I mouthed to Mary across the room. But Maureen was looking so serene and full of the Lord, it seemed wrong to do anything other than stay with her.

I cleared my throat: 'It's just God. She's OK. She's fine. Just wait and see.'

Mary added, 'Yes, we've seen it happen before,' omitting to add that we hadn't really known what to do then either.

Maureen stirred and sat up. She looked round with a contented smile on her face. Her exuberant character was, at least for a moment, stilled and she looked at peace with herself and the world. 'I don't know what happened,' she said, 'but I feel great. A sort of warm rosy glow came all over me. I felt sort of cocooned. It was lovely.'

I reassured the group. 'It's the Holy Spirit. Just like we've been teaching you.'

From the background another person spoke excitedly: 'I've got pins and needles all over my arm,' she said. Heather was one of a group of three women who had been praying for the 'right' new vicar during the time of interregnum. I believe it was as a result of their prayers that we received a prophetic word of scripture, simply saying, 'Come over to Macedonia and help us.' *(Acts 16:9)* Birmingham was to be our 'Macedonia'.

Heather is a lovely, unpretentious yet dedicated woman of God, and a great and increasing joy to us: a true gift from the Lord. Her hand reached up to her collar bone. She touched it gingerly and then with greater pressure. 'And I can't feel any pain,' she gasped.

Heather quietly shared her health problem: 'Calcium deposits have built up on the bone, so when I raise my arms above shoulder height, the left arm goes dead. There's no pulse either.' She went on to explain, 'It's been so painful I could hardly move my shoulder sometimes, and that bone area – well, I've not been able to touch it for years.'

Her excitement grew. 'Something's happened. I'm sure God's healing me,' she spoke out. 'Yes, he is. I can feel it. My shoulder feels as though it's on fire!'

Later, as I came to write this page, Heather confirmed: 'God started to heal me because I'd been obedient. I didn't want to stand up and pray with Maureen, but I knew God wanted me to. And because of my obedience, I believe he touched me with his healing.'

The group began to react. One or two looked unbelieving: was it all a 'put up job' by the vicar? Another shifted uncomfortably in his seat, while other members were looking distinctly thrilled: here was God alive and active.

After one or two Tuesday night 'specials', Mary and I were getting ready for revival.

'Look at what's happened after our prayers!' we exclaimed to each other feeling quite elated and superior.

So the following week we started to pray again. One couple stepped forward: we prayed... and absolutely nothing happened. Then another man... absolutely nothing. I smiled confidently at the group and said, 'Wait for the physical manifestation of the Spirit. Just wait and see...' Absolutely nothing.

The heavens were surely empty, as if a great heavy curtain was across the room. I felt totally drained and hollow. 'God! Why have you brought me this far only to let me fall?' Painful memories of the past flooded my mind, and I resolved in the heat of the moment to turn my back on him. 'That will show him!' I thought arrogantly.

As I reflected on this some days later, when the passion of the moment had died, the Lord gave me a supernatural understanding of the whole situation. I sensed God was saying to me, 'Wallace, the other week was just a dawning, a touch of my power. You wait and see what I will do.' It was as if God were giving a glimpse of how it could be.

But my job, for the time being, was simply to get on with building up his church. 'For we are God's fellow-workers,' *(1 Corinthians 3:9)* says St Paul as he begins his great exposition of God's building site. It is so necessary to build upon the true foundation of Christ rather than on seemingly delicious experiences of the moment, helpful though they sometimes are. As Paul reminds us, our true and lasting work will 'be shown for what it is, because the Day will bring it to light. It will be revealed with fire, and the fire will test the quality of each man's work.' *(1 Corinthians 3:13)* What God wants in his church, as well as the overnight sensation of experiential faith, is the ongoing hard toil of faithful listening, hearing and obeying. Back again to the Red Sea Syndrome. This needs to be a fundamental understanding for all Christians.

Later, God was to tell us of his plan for a specific 'building site' programme. However, in those early days we had to make do with a general understanding that we had just started on a laborious journey to build up the church. His power was upon us, and we were to be co-workers – with the emphasis on 'work'.

* * *

The telephone rang.

'Can I come and talk? Soon?' Maureen's excited voice trilled effervescently. 'I've got an idea I want to share with you, and I think it's from the Lord. It's really important.'

Inwardly I groaned. It's lovely to witness Christians develop a new dynamic of faith as they experience the Holy Spirit, but why do they seem to think they have a personal and exclusive hotline to God?

'Yes, Maureen, of course you can,' I answered. 'Come round to the vicarage tomorrow morning and have a coffee with Mary and me.' ('Best to have Mary there,' I thought. 'She'll keep our feet on the ground.')

Our golden retriever, Sarah, was very excited. She loves visitors. In fact she still tries to throw herself at everyone and lick them to death. She liked Maureen especially, and sat at her feet under the table ready to receive as much affection and as many biscuits as possible. But that day Maureen was too intent on her notion.

'I believe the Lord wants me to work full time at St Boniface's,' she blurted out. 'Not to be paid, but just to work for him here.'

'OK,' I responded cautiously. My mind was working overtime. Right through the Scriptures God delights to establish teams. Back in the time of my hero, Moses, as he battled with the Amalekites, all went well as long as Aaron and Hur were supporting him. Yet it is so easy to be tempted into the non-biblical pattern of the 'omnicompetent' vicar. Especially in areas where little lay leadership talent appears to be forthcoming.

'What's your reaction, Mary?' I said to gain time. But Mary was ready and waiting with her immediate answer.

'I think God's in this,' she replied. 'And I know your opinion of "omnicompetent" vicars. Well, here's a chance to start developing a team. Anyway, Maureen's already shown herself to be good at pastoring people… and it's not exactly your strong point.'

She was right.

'Maureen, if you do this, it'll have to be on proper terms. I'm not going to go easy on you just because it's a voluntary job.'

'Yes,' she agreed. 'That's how I see it. It would be a proper job, but my salary would be part of our stewardship. Why shouldn't it work well like that?'

I was flabbergasted. A full-time member of staff! No more lonely morning prayers. And how the work could be expanded, because Maureen had skills that, although undeveloped at that time, were complementary to my personal gifting.

'Right, you can start on Monday.'

Sarah jumped up and confirmed my comment as she attempted to steal Maureen's biscuit.

* * *

I sat quietly with Mary that evening.

'I don't know how I can hold this all together. One moment it seems that God is going to break out in revival, and then almost immediately it all goes as quiet as the grave. People "falling in the Spirit" at our Praise and Prayer, and then silence from heaven; Maureen offering herself full time today, but what about tomorrow? And the church itself: it's still absolutely locked into "churchianity", but I also sense something else in the air on Sundays. I don't know how to cope with all these contrasts.

'And look at what's happening out there. Things are more or less OK round the church, but those kids torched that stolen car in the Valley just yesterday.'

I shook my head. It was all too much.

'It's like you said to me the other day,' replied Mary. 'It's like a touch of God's power. Like a sunbeam on a winter's day.'

She was right. It's surely a characteristic of a church rising from slumber. So many chains still tying it down yet a sense of possibility.

I sat and considered how one of the first things that Jesus did in the early days of his public ministry was to set up a team around him: the twelve disciples, as well as all the other followers. It was as if the Lord was beginning to set up his team in Quinton.

I was so thrilled that at last Mary was able to develop her giftings in prophetic insight, teaching and leadership support – an amazing change from just a few months earlier. And now Maureen, as well as a growing number of followers, was on board. I sensed that Maureen would be far from the last of those offering themselves full time. And so it turned out to be. The exciting thing about working for God is that his agenda for church growth is not linear. It takes all sorts of unexpected dives and turns.

However, before God built up a larger team of very different personalities and giftings, we still had to go through the learning process of how to step out in faith: a seemingly very risky business…

7

Learning to Take 'Faith Risks'

Do not conform any longer to the pattern of this world.

Romans 12:2

'Shut your b*** mouth!' the mother screamed at the child, and dragged him across the floor of the church hall.

A helper didn't even bother to look up because the violence and the language were so normal. The other toddlers just got on with their games; this was what life was all about. In the kitchen cigarette smoke saturated the atmosphere, together with the smell of burned toast, as members of staff laughed together. On a side bench lay a heavily soiled disposable nappy amid the general clutter of equipment needed to run the children's playscheme.

The idea was to provide a break during the day for mums under pressure, most of whom were on the social services list. They could bring their children to the church hall to be cared for, so creating space for themselves. It was a good idea. A secular charity ran the scheme on behalf of the government to provide a much-needed social amenity and also invaluable work experience for people interested in childcare. Yes, it was a good idea.

The church was able to rake in the cash from the five-days-a-week letting. It had become a very important part of the budget and that meant we couldn't upset the hirers. 'Don't rock the boat,' I was firmly ordered by more than one church member. 'We can't manage without the income.' And I had to agree. We would soon become bankrupt without the extra money. And of course in the eyes of society it looked good: the church co-operating with a secular, well-meaning charity to help those in need.

'It's not right, is it?' I commented to Mary as we were driving towards the Welsh Marches on our day off.

'What are you talking about?' she enquired. She was confused because I'd dramatically changed the subject from family birthdays to my worries about the playscheme in our church hall.

'Do you know Maureen had to bring one of the toddlers back last Friday? He was running around outside in the pouring rain with nothing on except a tee-shirt, not even any pants. And when she took him back in, no one seemed to have even missed him.' I continued, now in full flow: 'And earlier last week there was a full potty on the kitchen floor as they were cooking dinner. It's absolutely incredible!'

I felt vaguely guilty, because here I was again discussing work. Mary would often say to me, 'Is there no escape?' One trouble with being a minister is that it's very difficult to mentally shut off from things. All the goings-on within the church fellowship need to be reflected upon, and prayed through. Sometimes I think it would be marvellous to pack up work at 6 p.m. or so and drive away, leaving it all behind till the next day – perhaps attending a Bible meeting in the evening or something completely different from the daily task. With ministry, I can never escape – even my house is full of church business.

Other times, I thank God for the tremendous privilege of being able to give myself completely to his work, 24 hours a day. It's positively helpful to chat with Mary because she is equally committed and I feel safe. I don't have to be guarded in case I make a stupid comment or throwaway phrase that some well - (or ill-) meaning church member may quote back at me sometime in the future.

But today Mary took up the conversation with gusto because she was incensed by the whole playscheme being given a good name merely because they used our hall. 'What about that mother who rang up the other day asking about the church nursery? I spent ages explaining it was nothing to do with us – we only hire out the hall. I don't think she believed me at all. Maybe she was right in a way, because it is our hall, and it's as if we're giving the playscheme our seal of approval. And have you seen how some of the mothers treat their children? All that yelling and screaming and swearing. I've seen quite a few of the mums hit their kids an awful lot. It does look as if the church accepts it all.'

'I don't know what I can do about it, Mary,' I complained gloomily. 'I'm fed up with continually protesting to the managers. But it doesn't make any difference. They don't seem to have any control over their helpers. And, of course, most of the children they look after have special social needs, so it's not that easy...'

The car in front unexpectedly pulled off sharply to the right, forcing me to brake hard. After some moments I commented resignedly, 'But I'm going to have to do something, aren't I?'

Mary nodded her agreement.

We drove along quietly on our way to Croft Ambrey, a lovely remote Iron Age fort not too far from Ludlow. I was looking forward to a stiff four-mile walk before lunch. It was Mary who raised the subject again.

'Wallace,' she said. 'You know, I think we're missing the point altogether. Never mind about the money or even the church's name; the important thing is it's not glorifying to God. That's what's wrong with it! That's why it has to be sorted out. I think you'll just have to close it down.'

It was all very well for her to say that, but it was me who would have to sort it out with the church council (PCC) and carry the financial can. I said aloud, 'But Mary, if I stop the playscheme, our finances will be completely up the spout. And they're bad enough already; Can you imagine what the PCC would say? They'll have kittens if I even suggest it.'

Mary smiled sweetly at me. 'But Wallace, you're always telling me that if God leads he will also provide. Don't you believe your own theology?'

Oh, the horrible logic of Christian Wives. I started to sulk, because there was no way of talking myself out of what had to be done.

* * *

I was right. The PCC were not happy.

'Stop the playscheme? How on earth do you think we are going to pay our bills if we do that?' was the immediate reaction.

'In for a penny, in for a pound,' I thought. 'So here goes.'

47

'I'm sure it's not honouring to the Lord,' I explained. 'It uses the name of his church, but they do whatever they want. It can't be right, can it?'

Maureen helpfully interjected, 'I know what you mean. The other week I was talking to one of the mothers and she was sure it was a church playgroup. She was complaining about things, and when I said that it was nothing to do with the church, she looked incredulous. And she's been going there for months now.'

I added, 'And while we're talking about church income, I really think we have to work out exactly what methods of income are honouring to God. Church members have to learn about right giving rather than always relying on jumble sales, fétes and so on. God wants his people to give from a sacrificial and generous heart. Surely this church has to run on faith and not that sort of fund-raising, otherwise we'll be spending all our time making money rather than proclaiming the gospel. Is that what you want?'

As I delivered my mini-sermon, it was clear by the various reactions that this was a new way of looking at church finances. People glanced at each other cynically, with wry smiles: 'Let's indulge him until he finds out about the real world,' you could almost hear them thinking.

'The playscheme will have to go,' I continued. 'It's bringing our church into disrepute.' The smiles started to tremble slightly.

'And we must begin to pay our full financial share to the diocese.' The indulgent smiles disappeared.

'And we can't let out the church hall on Sundays after all we've been saying about keeping Sunday special.' People started to shift in their seats. They saw the point, but could it possibly work out in practice?

'Vicar,' argued one of the members, 'people round here don't have much money, and everybody in this church is doing the best they can. I don't understand how you can ask us to give more. And the playscheme… well, it's been very good for us.'

There was a general nod of agreement. It's astonishing that individually church people can agree with faith concepts and even get excited about looking to the Lord in new ways, but the moment they come together as a council, faith flees and practicalities take absolute control.

'Well,' I declared, 'the Lord will have to grow the church so that more people are covenanting. God will have to bring more people into our church.'

There was a deadly silence.

'We've tried that before, but none of the folk round here are interested in the church.'

'And nobody from that new estate would ever come to this church,' said another 'solid' member. 'So what makes you think you can succeed where others have failed?'

'Well,' I persisted doubtfully, but words ran out. What could I say? I believed these lettings were not honouring to God, yet without them how could we raise the finances to run the church?

The silence became absolute.

* * *

In so many church council meetings, worldly sense spoken by the most able orator wins the day. I know that many leaders feel overwhelmed by a few who are able to dominate the proceedings. Some vicars find a stiff sherry the only answer! Yet the painful fact is that a leader has to lead.

There is no backing down from such a heavy responsibility unless the church is to flounder under godless monopolisation.

Pragmatism is a bad bedfellow for any Christian organisation. It means we can become wedded to prosaic reality rather than a vibrant Godward-looking faith. Yet how difficult it is to truly differentiate between blind irresponsibility and faithful conviction. The Christian has to make decisions that are honouring to God, and yet avoid presumption upon his grace. However, the biblical principle is utterly clear. Paul says, 'Do not conform any longer to the pattern of this world, but be transformed by the renewing of your mind. Then you will be able to test and approve what God's will is – his good, pleasing and perfect will.' (Romans 12:2)

The only question that truly remained in our playscheme situation was simply one of timing and presentation, coupled with prayer. The prayer could be provided by our emerging Praise and Prayer group; timing and presentation would be down to me. I sensed in the depth of my being that God was offering us an opportunity to get things right. It had to be grasped. This was the moment.

The treasurer, Bill Smith, was a longstanding member of the church. I put forward my propositions to him privately, adding, 'Bill, I know it seems daft to close down the playscheme and lose all that income, but it's not right, is it?'

He assured me, 'That's all right, Wallace. You must do what you believe God is telling you to do. Go ahead.'

I began to preach about faithful risks for God, quietly teaching faith principles. It was so important to work hard at ensuring the congregation grasped and owned the direction of my leadership. Some weeks later the PCC gave unanimous agreement. God had obviously been working on them through teaching, prayers and hard ongoing work. I wasn't sure they fully understood, but they had an inward sense of what was being taught – and even more important they were now willing to trust me.

I sat down and wrote the letter:

Dear Sirs,

We have decided not to renew your church hall letting. This reflects our growing concern about the management of the project. Despite our protests, no improvement has been forth-coming...

The letter went into the postbox and I breathed a sigh of relief. Even if it all went wrong, I knew I had done the right thing for the kingdom.

Sometime later, I wrote to the Sunday user:

I regret we can no longer let the hall on Sundays. We believe the Lord's day must be kept special and the church has to back its words with its actions...

With great trepidation, Bill and I sent off practically all our remaining funds to pay the diocesan share and loan repayment in full. 'Lord,' I questioned in my worried prayers, 'is it right to take this faith risk?'

Despite my doubts, I began to thank him that all would be well. And as my prayers turned into praise, I sensed his assurance flooding into my heart. The finances would be OK.

* * *

It was in the following December that the financial 'faith risk' principle came to its final test. I sat with the treasurer in his front room, coffee in hand, the church books laying in front of us. We were almost ready to do the year-end tally.

'Bill,' I said, 'it's a bit like being in the dentist's waiting room.'

'How do you mean?' he replied.

'Well, there's no escape, is there? We've got to do the books. But what if the money's all over the place? You know I'd have to resign or something?'

Bill merely raised his eyebrows as he reached out for the books, and then slowly sipped his coffee as he started to scan the figures. Together we worked things out: £500 allowance for fuel, but what about that rebate from the insurance people? Have we had all the tax back? Where does this figure fit in? And so it went on for about two hours.

Bill said it first: 'Do you know, I think we're going to be all right. It seems to be balancing. I don't quite understand where we've got all this income from, but here it is in black and white. And look at that gift of £800 – that's really helped.'

'It's OK, Bill,' I breathed with relief. 'We're OK!'

We had projected forward to the end of the financial year and would scrape in, almost to the pound. I sat back in contentment. 'That's amazing. Who would have thought it? We've lost all that income and yet we're solvent. God is good, isn't he?'

We reported back to the PCC. The members were absolutely delighted. I perceived that most of them really wanted to do things God's way, but had been afraid and needed permission and leadership to exercise faith. And it's particularly faith building to see God moving in his church, not merely in the obvious supernatural ways, but even within its finances. They saw how the books balanced without the usual fund-raising jumble sales and despite cancelling the various unhelpful hall bookings.

Perhaps for the first time some began to comprehend how the spiritual affects the physical. Others thought it a plain old-fashioned miracle!

Money dominates the agendas of so many church councils, and can lead to many ungodly 'discussions'. But we were learning together that church finance can be just as much under God's control as, say, spiritual healing. It's a matter of offering all things to him.

Over the following years our budgets have narrowly balanced; good housekeeping has been essential, together with proper financial control. Today we are able to give 10 per cent of our income to Christian charities.

We have also learned that one 'faith risk' leads to another... and another...

8

Barbed Wire and Wild Horses

Neither do people light a lamp and put it under a bowl.

I crept out stealthily, armed with wire cutters and helped by two burly church members.

'That barbed wire is coming down, whatever the consequences,' I whispered furtively.

They smiled and held it ready for the first cut... and our second major 'faith risk'.

* * *

The church complex was surrounded by barbed wire, ostensibly to keep vandals out. On the face of it, this was a sensible idea since the vulnerable flat-roofed building with unprotected windows proved to be a continually exciting target. However, this physical barrier also created a problem. The barbed wire symbolised the barrier between church and community. 'We don't really want your sort and your problems here,' it said. Noticeably the wire was thicker and more prominent next to the new estate, especially where the large rear gates stood forbiddingly padlocked together, topped with four strands of it. They said more clearly than any words: 'Keep Out' – not just to possible vandals but to the whole area.

I sat in the church one day with the doors locked, seeking God in prayer. He started to speak to me about the barbed wire. 'It must come down, you know. It's not right around my house.'

'But Lord, what will happen? Surely it will be like an open invitation: "All Vandals Welcome"?'

'That's my problem, not yours,' were the words that came into my mind. And I remembered the word Maureen had offered at one of our early Praise and Prayer meetings: 'A city on a hill cannot be hidden. Neither do people light a lamp and put it under a bowl.' *(Matthew 5:14-15)*

I always find the best way of prayer, for me, is simply to chat with God – to share with him how I feel. Of course, it takes faith to believe he is truly listening, but often ideas and concepts seem to pop into my mind and heart during those times. I have learned to discern the voice of God, though I do sometimes listen to my own emotions and thoughts, attributing them to the Divine. But if you never try, you never learn. Indeed, for many years I have gone to a local convent one day a week whenever possible, for peace and quiet. Often I have taken no reading material, save a Bible, and no agenda – not even a hidden one! Then I have simply offered the day to God. The first half hour is usually very slow – I nearly always have to pass through a boredom threshold. But I know I have to persevere. Then, as often as not, it all clicks together and I have that sense of sitting at God's fireplace – simply alongside him. Of course, checking out thoughts with the Bible is essential. As the day develops, I find a whole range of new thoughts opening up, and before I know it, the clock tells me that time's up.

Often it has been during those times that the Lord has spoken quite radically into my soul, and I can go home and seek to put it into action. And it's quite amazing how the consequential results seem to fit the situation so miraculously. I might not have an agenda, but my faith tells me that God certainly does! It goes back to that old song again: 'Turn your radio on... get in touch with God... turn your radio on.' Of course the 'radio' is our inner soul tuning in to God's voice. And it works. But practice makes perfect. You wouldn't expect a car mechanic to learn his trade overnight, and neither can a minister of the gospel learn to hear God without hard work, application and faith. We will never do great things alongside God without listening to his voice, and ministers have a calling on their lives to be people of prayer. Yet how often I notice that busyness supplants all things – or is busyness merely an excuse for not battling to hear God?

As I sat in church that day, I perceived the unremitting problem of the church hiding behind worldly protection rather than lowering its defence and becoming vulnerable – yes, even to vandals, but especially to the needs of the community. The problem is especially true of most churches on council estates on the outskirts of large cities. The buildings often have wired-up windows and sometimes a high-pronged fence surrounding hall and gardens. Many have walls covered in graffiti, looking gaunt and separate from the community. Like fortresses set up against the neighbourhood they were built to minister to, they send a visual, almost subconscious, message that the church has no answer to the problems of society; that God's church is merely part of the world and totally subject to its destructive powers. Whereas the wonderful, vibrant truth of our faith is that God can and will intervene according to his divine purposes and the prayers of his people. It is a scandal that some of today's church buildings are barricaded strongholds rather than bulwarks of truth for the population. The church must preach by its actions that there is a profound connection between the physical and the spiritual.

'Lord, you're right,' I affirmed. 'We can't sit in splendid isolation behind man-made barriers, however sensible they may seem to us.' I felt a growing sense of anger that the church had been forced into a defensive mode rather than leading in faith. However, I still had to spend a further two hours in prayer seeking to understand the difference between removing the barbed wire and, say, opening the church doors 24 hours a day with the maxim 'God will provide the security'. I saw the removal of the wire as my obedience to God's calling, which would have to be constantly backed up by intercessory prayer, whereas any other action would have been my presumption.

'I'll do it, Lord,' I confirmed as I finished my prayer time and went home for tea… carefully locking the church door behind me. This 'faith risk' just had to be actioned, with or without church approval.

Mary and I sat and formed a plan. I would creep out one evening with gloves and wire cutters, then afterwards I would face the repercussions from both church council and vandals. However, we stood at the edge of indecision for quite a few weeks. Should we or shouldn't we? Then God spoke through a remarkable 'coincidence'.

'I think the Lord is giving me a picture,' said the young man at the prayer meeting. Mary was speaking to an invited group from another Birmingham church, and I was leading the evening. 'I don't understand it at all,' he said. 'It looks as if Wallace is holding a large pair of wire cutters. Does that make any sense?'

Well of course it made total sense. 'Thank you, Lord!' we almost shouted out and then proceeded to share with them our dilemma regarding the prison camp atmosphere around the church.

Two nights later, I got together with those 'burly church members' and tackled the barbed wire. The large rear gates came off and an access was opened for the Valley to enter the church grounds. 'This isn't very Anglican,' I thought as I attacked the wire. 'No committees or steering groups or agreement from the PCC.' Later, as I lay in my bed tossing and turning, I imagined all sorts of repercussions. Perhaps letters sent to the bishop about my 'precipitous and rash action'; or the PCC in some way disowning me; or, even worse, the whole of the church complex being hit by local vandals, making my faith teachings totally null and void. At 3 a.m., following much sleepless tossing and turning, this faith venture felt like sheer folly. It seems to me that all people who seek to live by faith continually question their own actions. It's par for the course. Taking faith risks is not a comfortable way to live!

People were both pleased and displeased. Some clearly felt the consequences were now on the vicar's head – the best place for them to be. Others were excited about the 'picture' and consequent action, sensing God's leading. Some just shook their heads. Yet leaders sometimes have to get on and do things, taking the decision and the consequences. If Moses had waited for consensus before approaching Pharaoh with the famous words 'Let my people go', *(Exodus 5:1)* I suspect the Old Testament would have been significantly different. And if the Virgin Mary had said, 'Let me go and consult the rabbi,' rather than, 'I am the Lord's servant. May it be to me as you have said', *(Luke 1:38)* then perhaps the New Testament would never have come into existence! Of course it is arrogant foolishness for leaders to equate themselves with such people. But there is a strong biblical precedent that must be observed and obediently followed. Back again to our Red Sea Syndrome.

We have to beware presumption – one of the many reasons why building up a support team is so important. But in those early days I had to stand or fall by decisions made prayerfully with Mary. The Anglican Ordination Rite is helpful in this area. Would-be vicars are told, 'Because you cannot bear the weight of this ministry in your own strength but only by the grace and power of God, pray earnestly for his Holy Spirit.' We surely did not come into full-time leadership to spend most of our time being funeral directors, social workers or such like. They can be important ministries, but not the core of our calling. It is so easy for clergy to become slaves to the system instead of being free to follow God's direction. We are called to be leaders... and lead we must. The church is not a democracy but a theocracy, and God, I believe, mightily calls out his leaders to lead. It's important for us ministers to be pastors, enablers, encouragers, carers, shepherds, and so on, but primarily we are to be leaders of God's people.

Dramatic action can often provide an excellent teaching situation: it can rally feelings and reactions, and people become involved. Instead of being an argumentative item on the council agenda, the barbed wire became a gigantic visual aid about the church's responsibility to welcome people of all ages and all backgrounds into the Lord's house. Sharp action can be very effective when it has a root in God's calling, rather than merely following a vicar's pet idea. God's word about the wire cutters to that young man was the key.

Taking faith risks can be infectious. It wasn't long before the vast majority of the congregation became involved in a risk that was to give great fruit, as it radically reformed our Sunday worship. Indeed it indirectly changed the whole outlook of the church...

* * *

Worship was a bone of contention at St B's. We were beginning to grow a committed fellowship, especially within our smallish Praise and Prayer group. New and old Christians were learning to praise God in a different way and experience the power and presence of the Holy Spirit. But Sunday services were still quite dry, and hardly reflected the growing spirituality.

Maureen's constant question, 'Wallace, when are we going to experience "spiritual" worship on Sundays?' was a growing challenge. The services appeared to be bogged down in little red books of liturgy and traditional hymns Ancient and Modern... more ancient than modern I fancied. And the organ was king. For most people of our area, the slow ponderous music of the hymn culture was totally removed from normality, experience or possibility.

A visit to the newsagent at that time was very instructive. On the counter, papers were piled in height according to sale. *The Sun* had pride of place, followed by all the tabloids. There was one copy of *The Times* and two *Independents*... one of which was reserved for the vicar.

Visits to parishioners' homes were equally enlightening: books were not in evidence, but videos were, together with a room dominated by a blaring television set. Yet here was the church thrusting book after book into people's arms as they entered. 'The service this morning can be followed from page 119' – if indeed we were allowed to give page numbers. 'It's an intrusion on the dignity of our worship,' some would say. 'Keep one finger in page 120 and turn to page 127... open your hymn books at number 456... we omit verses seven and nine... please take your notice sheet home and don't forget to read it.'

The barbed wire might have been an external barrier, but we soon realised the church had built up its own internal barriers. It came as a shock to discover limited reading skills and that the imposition of a book culture was unhelpful, unacceptable and even insulting. It's interesting that the Christian Research Association found:

'40% of 21-year-olds reported difficulties with writing and spelling. If this means they also have problems reading, how do they cope when they come into a church and are expected to read, to sing hymns and read a liturgy?' *(Christian Research Association on 1992 social trends)*

Music was an even greater problem. If most people's living rooms were dominated by the television, the rest of the house echoed to popular music. Yet the church often insists on services dominated by an alienating type of music that is supposedly 'sacred'. Add to that a cerebral style of preaching and a non-personal form of presentation and weird robes, and it makes a cocktail that ensures the people of the area have to wade into and through a foreign wilderness of religious convention. Churches in the midst of such specific social trends, which continue to promote an unrelated, irrelevant and obscure culture, are committing cultural discrimination and need to re-examine Martin Luther's perceptive statement: 'If you don't address the key issues of today, you are not addressing any issues.'

These internal barriers have been very effective in killing estate churches. It is a fact that Anglican church attendance on the outer estates of Birmingham is now made up of fewer than four adults and one child per 1,000 population and decreasing. That means about 1,000 adults and fewer than 300 children attend those churches on an average Sunday from an overall quarter of a million population. In my observation most of those adult churchgoers are elderly, and the children are not, in the main, from church families. Some estate churches have no children at all! I'm told that at the beginning of the twentieth century about half the children in the UK attended Sunday school. *(All figures from 'The Hidden Poor', a report by Wallace and Mary Brown, 1996)*

Right across the nation, outer-council-estate churches are failing. It could only be an ostrich that refuses to see our depressed, 'siege mentality' churches with congregations of only a few score, huddled together for warmth, becoming strongholds against the community they are there to serve. Above everything else, they are not bringing people to vibrant faith. The figures speak for themselves. There is surely an enonmous need for a radical new approach if we are to proclaim the gospel of Jesus Christ fully to this generation.

In a report I compiled in 1996 I referred to those on the outer estates as 'the hidden poor', ('The Hidden Poor, Wallace and Mary Brown, 1996) not only to reflect obvious social need, but also the 'hidden' godlessness that pervades our outer estates. That hidden godlessness, that 'poorness' of spirituality, is the root cause of the disintegration of the estate churches and the terrible social problems arising. There is a sense of lingering death. Yet in the Birmingham area, new churches were built specifically to serve the new estates as the poor quality housing of the then inner city was torn down. The concept was stated in the early 1950s by Bishop John Leonard Wilson:

> New estates, well designed and spacious, are being swiftly built. But their inhabitants are strangers to one another, uprooted and often lonely. The estates are circles without centres For generations, strangers have become friends around the parish church... we are to live as persons in a society and not as units in a crowd. The new estates will make their full contribution to our way of life when they are communities with centres of worship and service. (Birmingham Diocese, 'Circles without Centres', 1951)

Today, many estate churches have failed to become centres of anything other than failure. We are heavily subsidised by the rest of the church, yet there is little vision and often an overwhelming sense of despair at not being able to do anything within the area we serve. And it's not just an Anglican problem. Other denominations also struggle in such areas, while 'new churches' appear to target areas with more obvious potential. Internal barriers ensure that churches remain stuck in a cultural time warp. 'Surely your God must be dead,' joked one man in the local pub. 'He probably died of boredom at having to listen to so many church services!'

* * *

It was during a Praise and Prayer meeting that God gave me a picture about developing relevant worship in church. It was a sort of illustrated concept in my mind's eye, which I then attempted to explain to the group: 'It's as if I saw a chariot fixed behind a team of wild horses. You know, like in Roman arena games. Only the horses were out of control – just galloping round and round, exhausting themselves and getting nowhere at all. The driver had given up and was merely hanging on.'

After a moment I went on: 'I think it's a picture of our church. God is showing me we're merely letting past events have their head and simply saying, "That's how we do things here." So we'll just keep going round in circles. Do you see?'

'I think I understand what you mean,' said one thoughtful member. 'Everything happens the way it does because it always has. If we could start with a clean slate in church, we might do things altogether differently. But we can't, or at least it seems we can't. So many things are already in place.'

'Yes, the past is controlling us today. Is that it?' questioned another.

Maureen stated uncompromisingly: 'We're stuck in a time warp. We've got to change with the times, but we can't seem to do it. It's like the organ.'

'What do you mean, "It's like the organ"?' I pressed her.

'Well, we've got an organist and an organ, and that's the way things are.' She smiled as if her bald statement were obvious to anybody with half a wit. 'Because he's there and turns up every Sunday, the services just sort of happen the way they do. And they always will unless we step in and take some radical action. After all, why should our services be dominated by unhelpful past ways, as if they were somehow God's ways?'

My job, I understood God was telling me, was to master those wild horses and bring the chariot back under control. Bringing St B's under God's authority would mean taking the reins with firmness and strength, turning the horses' heads and then quietly starting to follow his vision. It was no accident that the organ was mentioned. Our tentative endeavours towards relevant and suitable worship with guitar and singers were being impeded by sentiment. We had to retain the good and helpful, and yet draw strongly on the new spiritual songs the Spirit constantly inspires. And perhaps, more importantly, instigate a relaxation of strict Anglican formality. I was already starting to use the liturgy 'creatively', together with an overhead projector. But now was the time to fully develop an appropriate style for the people of the area we were seeking to serve. The church was not to be dominated by internal barriers of alienating written words, inappropriate liturgy and unsuitable types of music. Our resultant actions certainly provoked a reaction!

One older lady remarked, 'I think it's really disgusting. It's getting more like chapel here all the time.' Some folk used stage whispers to make critical comments during the songs: 'Whatever's he up to now?' they would murmur loudly as they refused even to look at the words. One couple stated: 'Well, he's not going to drive us from our church,' and kept up regular appearances just to prove a point.

Others were convinced that the robed choir had been the greatest strength of the church. Yet the 'new vicar' had scrapped the robes. 'If only we could build up the choir like it was in the old days,' they would remark. 'After all, it does bring the children into church and gives a certain style and dignity to the service.' How nostalgia can affect memory!

'I don't get anything from the music,' said a member at the next PCC meeting. 'It doesn't make me feel nearer to God. It somehow jars on me. I don't know why. Oh, he plays really well, but...'

'Here we go,' I thought. 'The guitar is just too much.'

Another lady quietly acquiesced. 'I didn't like to say anything, but I agree. Especially at the end of the service with all that highbrow discordant stuff.'

It occurred to my dull mind that they were not talking about the guitarist... but the organist!

'I can't stand that garbage, it gets right up my nose,' said one straightforward PCC member. All around people nodded their agreement. Encouraged by their assent he continued emphatically, 'We've got to tell him what we think of it and that it's not suitable for this church!'

My throat went dry at the thought of telling the organist anything. 'If I do that, I'm sure he'll resign,' I said weakly.

'Yes, what if he leaves and we're left without an organist? What would happen then?' questioned someone else.

'Well, I think the Lord wants us to use many more spiritual songs in worship,' said one of our keen members. 'And it seems to me that the organist doesn't even like them. So is he the right person for this church anyway?'

We prayed.

'I believe we have to send a letter telling the organist all our worries,' said the quiet lady. Slowly she unwound her thoughts: 'If he resigns, then so be it. God will sort it out. Like he did the money. We have to do what is right.'

The PCC agreed unanimously. I felt so excited. They had started to shoulder some of the undoubted burden that taking faith risks places on the initiator. But I also realised it was my teaching that had led them to this position. Suppose it all went wrong? Again the loneliness of leadership weighed heavily on me.

The letter went out in the next post and we held our breath. Soon we were to discover that God, given half the opportunity, can create a totally new direction. Already he had planned a divine response...

9

The Coming of Titus

But God who comforts the downcast, comforted us by the coming of Titus.

2 Corinthians 7:6

'MARY! MARY!' I shouted, loud enough to rouse everyone in the vicarage. Even the dogs became animated. 'Mary, they're coming!'

I burst into the kitchen. 'Martin and Janet have decided to come to St B's. Martin's just been on the telephone. Isn't that fantastic?'

Mary caught the excitement and we whooped around the now barking dogs. God was answering our prayers in a dramatic way by sending a couple to help us, just as we had asked him many times. Estate ministry can be very lonely for clergy and their family. It is true that we are surrounded by people, but few can offer 'peer' companionship. Leaders desperately need peer friends for personal support. How often we had sought God for folk with whom we had a natural affinity that could escalate into bonds of deep friendship.

After the initial enthusiasm died down, I continued, 'Martin said he believed God was calling them to work with us. That's what makes me so pleased. Why is it we only associate callings with ordained leaders?' I voiced my usual exasperation about clerical elitism.

'And isn't it great that God should bother with us!' Mary responded, as we went on to talk about the future.

Martin and Janet Knox, we knew even then, were God's particular gift to us. Janet was to be the direct answer to the church council's faith risk decision, and Martin was to bring a new dimension in developing our style of worship. Together they were to bring us personal encouragement and, most of all, comfort...

* * *

It had all started some months before.

'Wallace, please take that suitcase upstairs. How many times do I have to ask you?' Mary was not in the best of moods on arriving home from our summer holidays.

'Hang on a second, won't you!' I replied with exasperation and a touch of anger. 'I can only do one thing at a time!' I should have been refreshed and vitally ready to get on with things. But instead I felt jaded, trapped and tired.

'And don't forget to hang up your coat!' Mary's voice floated from the kitchen. I mouthed some silent unchristian words and sat down on the bed.

The telephone rang. 'Oh no,' I thought. 'I've only been home a few minutes. Give me a chance, won't you?' But I'm a compulsive telephone answerer, so downstairs I ran and lifted the receiver.

'You won't know me,' said the voice at the other end. 'My name is Martin Knox and I'm calling from Sheffield. I've just got a new job in Birmingham. Janet and I are Christians and we've been praying that the Lord will direct us to the right church.' Martin went on, 'Three people have suggested your name. Can we come and see you?'

How easily tiredness, apathy and even bad temper can leave you when something other than emptiness replaces it.

The following afternoon, they sat in the vicarage living room. Martin spoke with enthusiasm: 'We believe God wants us to work with the poor and needy. So we want to find the right church, buy a house and then work from the inside.' He continued ardently: 'Janet and I are looking round several areas, to find the right place. We're sure God wants us to be in a council estate area, but...' Martin's voice trailed off as it became obvious we were one of his 'test' areas.

As we walked round the parish with them, I could feel the joy of true Christian fellowship and even the root beginning of a soul friendship. 'Look at that garage,' indicated Mary as we trudged from the Valley. 'A short time ago the door was painted, showing a witch, complete with broomstick, who lived in that maisonette over there. And that house... it's the place where a social worker was murdered.'

I pointed to another house: 'The children in there, their mother's just gone to jail. She used to lock them in and leave them all night. We only found out through their terrible behaviour at school. I don't know what's happened to them now. But what a mess, isn't it?'

Mary said, 'And we've heard that three covens meet round the Valley area. So it's some place you're thinking of coming to live in.'

Martin looked excited and Janet looked dubious.

On our return, I opened the church door and we entered. It was a lovely summer afternoon and the building was warm and welcoming. We knelt down as a foursome in front of the communion table. What a poignant moment that was. Even then, I saw God was smiling his 'gift' onto Mary and me. But Martin and Janet had to decide for themselves, so I made no comment about my personal discernment.

The following Thursday, Martin rang. He simply said, 'I believe God wants us to join you at St B's. Can we call and explain everything next week?'

Some days later, as we sat in the vicarage, Martin quietly confided, 'During my prayers, I've sensed God speak into my heart, "You need to be in Quinton." As simple as that.'

But I knew that with Martin's legally trained brain it would not be quite so simple. He produced a list of 22 reasons why he and Janet felt God was calling them to Quinton: at the top was the fact that three of their Sheffield friends had suggested St B's.

'How they ever knew about it, I don't know,' Martin commented. 'But do you know the main reason?' he said finally. 'You both said, "Let's find out what God wants," and didn't just grab us merely to swell your church members.'

Martin remarked to me later, 'It all added up in a surprising and positive way.'

Three months later they moved into a small ex-council house on the estate. Hardly suitable accommodation for the new assistant city solicitor of the Birmingham Corporation. The house they chose sums up Martin's personality very well. Simply stated, he has a missionary heart. And this is reflected by his Bible-believing Christian lifestyle, use of money and time, even the choosing of his friends.

If only more Christians would follow his and Janet's example: moving into the heart of a needy area, ready to give of themselves. I'm sure God is waiting to bless many ministries (not just ordained) as people seek to follow him right into the midst of social needs. I get angry that many Christians 'love' the poor and deprived only from a distance. It's so conditional and surely doesn't reflect a Lord who lived and died in the midst of his people. The missionary spirit has created spectacular opportunities right across the globe during these last two centuries. Today there are wonderful missionary possibilities in the council estates of our major cities. Jesus said, 'The harvest is plentiful, but the workers are few. Ask the Lord of the harvest, therefore, to send out workers into his harvest field.' (*Luke 10:2*) The estates are ripe for harvest, but where are the workers? Where are the self-sacrificing Christians who are willing to commit themselves to 'incarnational ministry'? Is the shortage because we have separated ministry into lay and ordained? Many now think of full-time ministry as describing only those who are paid by the church or 'living by faith'. The people of God need to wake up to the fact that all Christians are in full-time ministry. Churches in difficult areas are often in dire need of committed Christians to work alongside the often overwhelmed leader. Where are all these people? Are they too busy enjoying their super-spiritual big churches to personally care for the poor and needy?

Another blessing followed. In fact the first of many from Janet, as her remarkable knowledge of the Lord's mind through the Bible bears fruit time and time again. Her Christian background furnishes a valuable framework of faith, hope and love which frequently overspills onto those around her. She gave us a Bible reading she believed was for us from the Lord: 'For when we came into Macedonia, this body of ours had no rest, but we were harassed at every turn… But God, who comforts the downcast, comforted us by the coming of Titus.' (*2 Corinthians 7:5-6*) How could she have known about our original

Macedonian vision? How could she have known how bad things had been for Mary and me at St B's? How could she have known that their arrival comforted us as Titus' arrival comforted Paul those many centuries before?

Oh, how the church needs 'the coming of Titus'. Where are all the Tituses of the twenty-first century?

Many other blessings have followed over the subsequent years of working together. Two in particular spring readily to mind. One autumn, the Knox family spent a holiday in western Scotland. On their return, we ate supper together, and Martin said, 'We had a real chance to seek the Lord last week.'

I looked up with my mouth full of their Islay cheese as Janet continued: 'It was all about commitment. To each other, to the Lord, but especially to you two. God underlined, once again, that he sent us to be a support to you. And that's what we want to be. That's right, isn't it Martin?'

The other instance was during a time of great personal trauma. I had to ask a person to leave the church for reasons that were confidential. I painfully kept my priestly vow of silence, but the other party propagated lies. Consequently I was being criticised by some in the church and many in the community. It was so good to have a prayer partnership with Martin and Janet where I could share my pain without them trying to winkle out the bottom line. I could trust in their total support. It was brilliant. Let me tell you, vicars need friends!

Church life was undergoing radical change. Not only was a new worship style slowly emerging, but unchurched people were beginning to drift in. God was allowing a diversity of congregation that I was very anxious not to turn into a divided congregation.

Early signs of Holy Spirit renewal meant some people were being blessed by the services: 'Great, wasn't it?' they would smile at me over coffee. Others, with equal candour, said, 'I know we have to change with the times, but I find all these new ways very difficult. I wish we could have the sung Gloria. I do so like it.' People were careful to sit in the 'right' part of the congregation, ready either to purse their lips during 'those awful choruses', or to lift their hands in worship. I continued to teach about the riches of diversity and the poverty of division. Slowly the groups were finding common ground in the Lord – if not in their own personal preferences. Underpinning the whole, was our weekly prayer meeting.

* * *

'Watch out! He'll have the candlesticks over,' yelled one concerned lady who was more used to children being seen and not heard in church. But the unchurched families had a different attitude and their youngsters ran round and round, through the sanctuary and even waving their hands from the pulpit. We were delighted to see all the newcomers, but some of the behaviour was appalling. The norms of so-called church behaviour are not the norms of the estates. Yet we knew a warm welcome and plenty of encouragement were dramatically important. Many of these people had been so rejected in other parts of life that one wrong glance could destroy.

A young unmarried mother with purple streaked hair and a live-in boyfriend said to me, 'I couldn't believe how people came and welcomed me. And nobody stared. I hadn't expected church to be like that.'

'I love this church,' said a neatly dressed white-haired lady, 'and what is happening is right. Church has to change like everything else. But Vicar, I do find it all so difficult.'

Yet within quite a short time, some of our 'respectable' ladies were caring for the needy. Others, I have to say, remained aloof and severely criticised me for 'ruining their church'. However; most of the congregation began, through teaching and personal sacrifice, to see the new and often smelly children through Christ's eyes: 'Let the children come to me, and do not stop them, because the Kingdom of God belongs to such as these.' (*Mark 10:14, GNB*) I notice, as I travel around other outer-estate churches, that children are often not welcome. This is no surprise given the figures quoted elsewhere. Children are OK in principle, as long as they don't affect the traditional style of worship. It is a paradox that many churches long to encourage other age groups, yet feel unable to sacrifice their ways in order to accommodate the unchurched.

Then there was the matter of music in worship and especially the PCC's faith risk... 'We feel your style of music does not fit well with the way forward for St Boniface's...' ran the letter sent from the church council to the organist. We had a good idea his resignation would come by return post. And it did!

I showed the organist's reply to Mary and said, 'What on earth are we going to do? I know it's right, but what's going to happen at the end of the month when his notice expires?'

I didn't wait for her reply because I knew it would be something like, 'Well, the Lord will provide. Isn't that what you're always teaching us?' I could do without that sort of holy comment as I searched my address book for some stand-in organists.

'Who can I ask?' I thought, but not one relevant name came to mind. I was mildly panicking.

On the following Thursday, Mary and I were helping the Knoxes move into their new house. In the hallway a guitar case protruded from a miscellaneous pile of objects. My attention was immediately rivetted.

'Does one of you play the guitar?' I asked as we sat for a cup of tea.

'Oh, didn't I mention it?' replied Janet. 'Sorry, I thought I'd told you. I was one of the musicians at our previous church in Sheffield.'

'Do you play the organ as well, Janet?' My heart thudded with anticipation.

'Yes,' she replied, 'but I play the piano much better.'

Mary blurted out our immediate need within the church. '... And it all happened the day before yesterday,' she ended with incredulous amazement.

Two Sundays later, Janet led the worship in church. What astonishment there was as she sat on the organ stool for the first time, and I explained to the congregation how God had answered the faith risk of the church council. Her sensitivity to diverse needs became a building point for the future direction of worship, and has enabled us to develop a band.

Someone proudly boasted, 'And we weren't without an organist for even one week. It must be God's provision. He must care for St B's.' His views reflected the feelings of the entire congregation.

* * *

As I've said before, the Anglican ministry can be a very lonely place, especially when one becomes a vicar for the first time. There is a sense of profound isolation that is terrifying: you are with so many people, yet not really one of them; conversations will suddenly stop as you enter the room; people start acting in strange, uncharacteristic ways; easy words in casual conversations take on great significance to some around you.

The loneliness was most noticeable on Sundays, standing in front of the congregation, some of whom were quite antagonistic. I was separated by position, robes, calling and expectations. 'Oh, not him again,' I sensed some people were thinking as I wearily walked to my stall.

'Welcome to St Boniface's, if this is your first time…' the same old words repeated themselves. '"In the name of the Father, Son and Holy Spirit"… please be seated.' Not only was I leading every week, but preaching too – until I was fed up with the sound of my own voice. But presumably not as fed up as the people who had to sit and listen. I have since discovered that nearly all churches on council estates are in this position. As I've already commented, few 'able' people choose to live on the estates, and it's unheard of for clergy to retire to such an area.

I did have one preacher at St B's. He was an older, godly man called Stan Cooper, who had been at the church almost since its beginnings in the 1950s. Stan was held in love and respect. Unfortunately for me, he was elderly and frail, so unable to be a great support in actual up-front ministry. So it was with immense joy that I discovered Martin was a Reader.

The first time Martin and Janet visited St B's, Stan was giving one of his increasingly rare sermons. 'I remember he preached a good evangelical sermon on the Upper Room,' commented Martin some four years later. 'Do you know,' he continued, 'the second time we came, you announced his death and prayed for his widow Kath. I remember feeling a special bond with him. And the third time, you presented a Diocesan Readers Award to Kath. I think it was for the longest serving Reader in Birmingham. I remember reflecting that every time I came to the church, Stan's name was somehow mentioned. I wondered why it should happen like that.'

He smiled. 'Then, do you remember how Kath came up to me a few Sundays later, and said, "Martin, I'd like you to have Stan's old robes!"?'

Stan's widow thought, as did most of the congregation, that Martin was a gift from God coming in the footsteps of Stan. Across the whole spectrum of the congregation, Martin was seen to bring the Lord's reconciliation between old and new – just as Stan had done before him. 'I really like Martin,' I often heard folk remark. 'He's like a breath of fresh air. He's so full of life and vitality.'

I suddenly and remarkably found that I could now be part of an up-front team. It gave a new freedom that meant we could start to develop our leading of worship to suit the needs of the area, as well as enjoying preaching mutuality. Together we could do it!

* * *

The church, I felt, was beginning to take root. It was founded on our regular commitment of Praise and Prayer at the vicarage on Tuesday nights. But other factors were starting to come together: I had the beginnings of a daily team with Mary and Maureen; people of the area were coming to faith; there was a growing sense of purpose and vitality in our Sunday worship, with another team developing between Martin and myself; and Janet was growing our music ministry. It began to have the feel of a church on the move.

Yet it was all so wobbly and transitory. The fellowship felt like a building made out of a pack of cards which could collapse at the slightest breath. We desperately needed some sort of strengthening. But how was that to come?

10

'The Tower is Falling Down...'

I was glad when Stephanas; Fortunatus and Achaicus arrived,
because they have supplied what was lacking.

1 Corinthians 16:17

The following is an extract from Mary's diary:

> Elizabeth staggered into the kitchen this morning looking
> totally overwhelmed. I saw straight away she was deeply
> disturbed. 'Mum,' she said, 'I had this funny dream. I saw our
> church quite clearly... it was so real... but the tower was falling
> down.' She looked anxious. 'It was as if it didn't have any
> strength. I wanted to shout at someone, "Do something about it!
> Don't let it all fall! You need to put some scaffolding up!"'

The interpretation clicked into Mary's mind during our day off some
weeks later. 'God wants to put his scaffolding up. Isn't that exactly what
we'd do if our church tower needed to be repaired... put scaffolding all
round it? Do you see? That's what the dream's all about.'

I didn't reply. Driving is a good excuse to avoid instant answers.

Later, we sat down for lunch at a pub in Colwell, a little village in the
Malvern Hills. I said, 'What do you mean by scaffolding? There's
nothing wrong with the church tower as far as I know.'

Mary lifted her eyes as if to say, 'Isn't it difficult when you have an
unimaginative husband to deal with, even if he is a vicar?' She went on,
'It's not the real tower. It's symbolic. The tower just represents the
fellowship at St B's. God is acknowledging that it's weak and needs

strengthening. So he wants to put scaffolding around. Have you got it now?'

I got it all right. And it was already starting. Maureen and Robert, Martin and Janet, and of course Mary and myself. Yes, we were to be his scaffolding, together with others God would send.

On our return, I quickly phoned the Knoxes and the Stands. 'Can we meet together on Sunday night?' I enthused. 'Mary and I are wondering if God has given us a concept for the leadership structure of St B's. We want to share it with you.'

The following Sunday, we sat together in the Stands' lounge and I explained Elizabeth's picture and our interpretation. 'You see, he wants to form a scaffolding to support the real church as it's being built up. He wants us to be that scaffolding.'

Martin grasped the possibilities immediately and replied excitedly, 'Yes, I can see exactly what you mean. And it fits so well with what I believe. We have to lead and teach church members to be church. I think it's amazing.'

Robert joined in enthusiastically: 'The idea of us being scaffolding while the people are being built up is so simple and yet so profound. Why hasn't anybody else ever thought about it... or have they?'

The concept of scaffolding is different from team building. In the outer-estates situation there are few competent or established and enabled leaders, although there are many with such potential, buried beneath difficult backgrounds. 'Scaffolding' meant the establishment of a principle of surrounding the often disempowered people from the estates with a support system within which, over the years, an indigenous church structure could be set up and empowered.

There and then we decided that God wanted the six of us to be a Ministry Support Team for St B's: 'scaffolding' the fellowship as it grew, as well as supporting me in leadership. And it all fitted in so well with my continual prayers for help in ministry. However, God wasn't prepared to leave the number at six, as we almost immediately found out...

The following Sunday, I looked around as I was preaching. Yes, there they were again. That made three services in a row. The young man looked enthusiastic and they both raised their arms during the worship. I sought them out afterwards.

'Hello. Nice to see you. Are you from around here?'

Richard replied, 'Well nearly, we live about three miles away.'

'So what brought you to St B's?' I questioned. Had fame suddenly come upon us, or had they lost their way? Casual visitors are rare.

'It was the A—Z. We've just moved to Birmingham so we looked for little crosses on the A—Z and here we are.'

St B's had been the first church on their hit list and, as it turned out, the last!

'When we stopped outside to pray, we knew this was it.' His wife Mary looked so pleased as she told me the story. 'It's where the Lord wants us to be. We knew before we even set foot inside.' It was characteristic of this lovely Christian couple that they expected God to speak to them clearly and straightforwardly, and so often he did. The Red Sea Syndrome of listening, hearing and obeying, which we had discovered almost by accident, was already a living reality in their lives.

So it was that Richard and Mary Chamberlain became valued members of our Ministry Support Team, later moving into the parish itself. Mary became a full-time pastoral assistant, and after two years' service at the Birmingham City Mission Richard joined the staff as a full-time mission assistant. At that later stage, both lived 'by faith' since the church was far from able to support them financially. I was delighted to note that their idea of living by faith was not invalidated by living on state benefit, as it seems to be with so many.

The scaffolding was growing, which was wonderful, but I constantly found Richard a challenging man to work with. He ceaselessly asked fundamental questions and I felt exasperated at having to re-examine almost everything. And he always seemed to have a different view from my logical conclusion. Later I was to value his stimulating attitude and understand how it widened our perspective in a most helpful way. And Mary was a wonderful, caring woman who was determined to live for Jesus.

Mark Santer, the Bishop of Birmingham, wrote in a visitation report:

There is particular cause for thanksgiving for the fact that... a team of committed men and women have gathered round [Wallace] and Mary so that he no longer suffers from the loneliness which is felt by many clergy who work in similarly demanding neighbourhoods.

He went on to talk in the same report of the rootedness of the Ministry Support Team within the parish:

I sense that the leaders of the congregation, together with their parish priest, have committed themselves to the neighbourhood in a way which is securely and positively anchored in the tradition of the local parochial ministry. This can properly be described as an incarnational kind of ministry. I do not underestimate the costliness of this approach.

Bishop Mark had rightly seen the self-giving of the Ministry Support Team, enabling them to work as scaffolding to the growing fellowship. However, there was still another piece of scaffolding to come...

* * *

'No dinner, no breakfast, no chocolate biscuits and no lunch for you,' said Mary with just a hint of triumph in her eye. The chocolate biscuits were the real sacrifice: I rarely survive a day without one (or two).

I retorted, 'It's not so bad for you. You don't mind fasting 'cos it will help your slimming. It's a much bigger offering for me. Anyway, I work harder than you...' She rolled her eyes meaningfully at our daughter and I hurriedly retreated from the kitchen to sulk in private.

The Ministry Support Team had decided to call a day of prayer and fasting to initiate a faith venture. We believed God wanted to grow a vibrant youth work and so had applied to the Church Urban Fund for finance to employ a youth pastor. However, we were very wary about developing a dynamic youth work before the church itself was spiritually vigorous and thus able to receive and welcome them. The pastor's job was almost pre-evangelism to the church body: to prepare us in our thinking and attitude so that young people could really find their place in the body of Christ through us. At the same time, the pastor would have the vicarage children and Maureen and Robert's children to practise on!

Unknown to us as we prayed and fasted, Martin and Julie Thompson were seeking God about their future. Martin felt sure that God wanted him to be a missionary, and his eyes were firmly fixed on Africa. His one doubt was how he could master the new language that would be required. Through a connection with an evangelical trust, Martin was invited to speak at St B's for the Harvest Celebration. I was amazed to find myself pointedly telling him that we'd just received funding from the Church Urban Fund for a youth pastor.

He retorted, 'You're not thinking of me, are you? I've got no thoughts whatsoever in that direction. God has called me to be a missionary.'

The following week Martin rang me. There was the sound of excitement bubbling as he spoke. I hadn't a chance to interject even one word before he said, 'At last night's prayer meeting, the minister read from Ezekiel 3. Do you know what verse 5 says? "You are not being sent to a people of obscure speech and difficult language." You see, I've always longed to be a missionary. But maybe I can be a missionary in Quinton and not Africa as I thought. Can I come and see you?'

The Ezekiel reading, together with a personal 'word', was enough for Martin. The Thompsons arrived some two months later. They were to give a great gift of prophetic insight into the leadership of the church.

Of course, prophets are often enigmatic people to live with through facets of everyday life. Martin spent so much time mulling over each and every decision and constantly asked, 'Wallace, do you feel you've really prayed about this?' with the obvious implication! I had yet to learn the need to accept people's spirituality and lifestyle as equal, if not better, than my own. Like Richard, I found Martin a challenge, yet also very, very stimulating. God, it appeared, was building a scaffolding of very diverse characters.

* * *

It would be easy for me to say that that was the end of the story – to say that God had successfully built up the scaffolding and everything in the garden was rosy. But life rarely takes on that fairy story identity.

I think the trouble came out of my own pride. I was so full of God bringing to us the Chamberlains and the Thompsons that I decided to take another man, recently converted, into the scaffolding, with painful results. He came from a difficult family background and was born and bred in the area. To me, the last point was very important because I so wanted to encourage indigenous ministry.

There can be no doubt he brought a new dimension into the Ministry Support Team, and we all considered it was important to foster leadership from the area. But the experience ended very painfully indeed, with a major moral issue. In the end I had to ask him to leave the team. He also chose to leave the church.

Why do such things happen? I certainly hadn't prayed things through before taking this man on, but then God is not vindictive. Perhaps the Ministry Support Team weren't ready to disagree with me at that point. Perhaps I 'spiritualised' the appointment by saying, 'This is what God requires.' Perhaps I brought him into leadership too quickly. Perhaps, perhaps, perhaps. I honestly don't know. But I do know it's very important to seek to build up teams to share the burden of ministry. I also know that many leaders feel let down by people they have trusted. I'd invested much time and emotion in this man's personal development. It's hard to accept being despised and rejected, but that's often part of the cost of leadership.

In the narrow world of church leadership there are many people you feel have plenty of potential and yet leave a sense of unease. It is easy to appoint elders simply because they are available and eager, but there is the much bigger issue of God's calling, which shouldn't be sidelined for the sake of expediency. I've spoken to quite a few vicars who regret the appointment of, say, a churchwarden, having discovered that the solving of an immediate problem has escalated into an even bigger one. Spiritual leadership calls for God's choice of people; very difficult if you minister among the disempowered.

Teams have such wonderful biblical precedence; they are essential. Paul says of the emissary team from Corinth who supported him: 'I was glad when Stephanas, Fortunatus and Achaicus arrived, because they have supplied what was lacking... For they refreshed my spirit and yours also. Such men deserve recognition.' (*1 Corinthians 16:17-18*) Our team was complete for the moment: Maureen and Robert Stand, Martin and Janet Knox, Richard and Mary Chamberlain, Martin and Julie Thompson and, of course, Mary and myself. It was strange that all were married couples in an area where relational instability is the norm.

* * *

The Ministry Support Team was complete, but God had another blessing to bestow. It was the newest man who initiated it. Things were falling apart for him and yet he was still able to hear God. 'I really believe God wants us to have a music keyboard and he's going to give us one by Christmas,' he prophesied.

At the back of the church sat a couple on their first visit. Richard and Viv Flowerday had been in Birmingham for about six months, but still hadn't found a home church. As the word 'keyboard' was mentioned, their ears pricked up. Richard had been asking God how and where to use his personal musical gifting, together with the keyboard he had just purchased. Some weeks later, Richard offered himself and his keyboard to the music ministry, expressing his own love of the Lord through his musical talents. In addition, Viv added her lovely spirituality and vocal talents.

The Bishop of Birmingham wrote in that same visitation report previously mentioned: 'The worship which is offered in church is lively and relevant to the needs of the neighbourhood. The music is particularly good.'

11

'They Empty the Bins on Mondays!'

Taking the very nature of a servant.

Philippians 2:7

Debbie threw herself dramatically on her mum and started to shriek. For a little girl of only two years, the rowdy pack of dogs chasing down the alleyway was too much to cope with. She was terrified.

Janet Knox scooped her up and took an involuntary step backwards. She too found the wild, unkempt and sometimes fierce dogs that roamed the Valley to be quite intimidating.

'What are they doing up here, away from the Valley?' she thought in the split second before she instinctively reacted to the situation. 'Of course! It's Monday. They empty the bins on Mondays!' But even as the thought took root she found herself falling backwards, Debbie clutched in her arms. Her body twisted round, smashing her precious daughter onto the concrete. The moment seemed to last for ever: she simultaneously felt and sensed Debbie's leg contorted at an odd angle. The dogs were pushing past her, oblivious to her presence, much more interested in the contents of the rubbish sacks at the end of the alleyway. But her real concern was for her child as shock began to run through mind and body.

'Debbie! Debbie!' she cried as she picked herself up and tenderly stroked her daughter. 'Are you all right, my love?'

But the words seemed foolish even as they left her mouth, because clearly Debbie's leg was broken. And badly broken, dangling limply. The little girl's shriek of terror turned first to astonished silence, then to screams of anguish and pain as the tears started to flow.

'Come on, let's get your leg seen to,' Janet comforted her, with more assurance than she felt.

The nurse at the hospital was extremely kind and sympathetic. 'We'll soon get you fixed up, love,' she said to Debbie with a competent smile. However, as she turned to Janet her smile dropped and she explained, 'I think it's quite a complicated fracture. She'll probably need to be in traction and plastered right up to her waist. How did it happen? It's quite an unusual break.'

Janet explained about the dogs and falling backwards and the nurse looked sympathetic. 'Oh, that's horrible. Well, I expect the doctor will be round shortly. So just let me have your details and then we can get organised. Now, what did you say your name and address was?'

Janet gave her name, and then started the address. But as she mentioned the name of the council estate, the look on the nurse's face changed abruptly. If a face could tell a story, hers would have written a book.

'Oh!' she exclaimed. 'Can you hang on a second please?'

Off she rushed-for a hurried conflab with her colleague, both of them looking over their shoulder at Janet and Debbie as they talked.

They returned together. 'We think the paediatrician ought to have a look at your daughter,' said the first nurse. 'Just to make sure, you know, that everything's all right.'

Her colleague nodded agreement, but glanced at Janet in an odd way. The atmosphere had cooled to almost freezing point.

'And Jenny will stay with you and Debbie – just to be on the safe side.' Janet was getting quite worried. From the way they were behaving a problem had obviously developed. But what?

Then it occurred to her: 'They think I've abused Debbie. They think I've hit her or something and that's why she's got a broken leg.' The thoughts hurtled through her already bruised mind with the force of an express train. 'It's because of my address! That's why they're calling the paediatrician in.' She felt dirty and distressed.

'Oh, Martin, it's so good to see you!' Janet flung herself at her husband as he entered the Ward. Martin looked very smart in his city clothes, carrying a briefcase. She blurted out the story. 'And I'm sure they think I've done it to her,' she cried out. 'Just because we live on that estate.' Martin put his arms around her and simply held her tight. Then they sat quietly together talking it through, Janet releasing her pent-up feelings and Martin his anger and indignation that his wife and child should be treated so shabbily just because of where they lived. Janet said to me later, 'I felt I had been judged to be a poor mother by the fact of living on the Valley. That, on top of the traumatic experience with the pack of dogs and Debbie's subsequent accident, was too much.'

Martin and Janet (as previously mentioned) were part of the 'scaffolding' called to live incarnationally on the estate. And here they were, finding out at first hand the inbuilt prejudices that certainly exist, sometimes with very good cause. They felt they were being stereotyped because of an address. Fortunately they were able to cope with the developing circumstances: both are 'empowered' because of background, education and financial status; they are 'successful' products of the prevalent postmodernist culture. However, if one of our inadequate lone-parent mothers from the estate had been in the same situation it could have spelled disaster. She would have had little confidence in herself to fight off the establishment and no husband (or even partner) to support her.

Later, Martin and Janet learned that the sort of injury Debbie had sustained was completely consistent with child abuse. In fact the fractures could not have resulted from a simple accident, but had to have had an outside force as the causal agent (in this case, Janet's own body as she fell). Martin sagely comments, 'But it's all part of the cost, isn't it? It's about giving ourselves into the area, working from the inside and experiencing what the people round here do. And it's not just in the obvious way. Whoever would have thought that being half-accused of child abuse could be the cost of Christian commitment to an area? It's amazing I think.'

Certainly we have discovered there is a real and unexpected cost to living and ministering in such areas. Another couple from our Ministry Support Team soon found this out...

Richard and Mary's ministry was going well. They had established and maintained a simple lifestyle so they could give themselves to the people of the area. Recently, they had opened their home to 'difficult' neighbourhood children, offering biscuits, care and Jesus. 'Richard, do you know that little Ronnie's mum has walked out again?' Mary would reflect to her husband. Or, 'Estelle's "uncle" has been at it again. I don't know what we can do. What do you think?'

Lately they had been shocked by a family with six children living in a three-bedroomed house. The eldest daughter had decided that she needed a room of her own, so the rest of the children all slept on mattresses on the floor in the boxroom. The parents were scared of the daughter and her violent temper, allowing her to dominate the house and family... even at 15 years of age. The two youngest boys were physically stunted and emotionally crippled.

Richard and Mary's trust in the children they sought to help was about to be tested.

* * *

'And don't use too much water, Nancy,' said Mary as she and Richard carefully instructed their friend on the care of the treasured house plants. Mary had trained as a botanist and Richard as a horticulturist, before hearing God's call to work among the poor and needy in the city. Both loved their exotic flora, and had taken great care over its management before leaving for a much needed holiday.

Their holiday cottage had been lent to them by a friend, while someone else had lent them a car. It's hard to 'live by faith' and continually accept charity, however well meaning. But that's part of the price when being released into their sort of ministry.

As soon as they arrived at the cottage, the telephone rang.

'Yes?' answered Richard, hoping perhaps it would be a wrong number.

'Richard, it's Nancy here,' said the distant voice with a slight tremble. 'I'm really sorry, but your house has been burgled.'

Her voice quivered even more as she told them how the baby's nursery bedroom had been vandalised. 'Oh, it's such a horrible mess! Poor Hannah!' she exclaimed.

Mary C. told me afterwards, 'It's not so much what was stolen, but the terrible sense of intrusion. It's as if they invade your personal space. It's a really terrible feeling.'

Later, they talked with the police. 'It had to be children,' the constable remarked. 'The window was tiny. Only a small child could have squeezed through. And that's how they got in.' He sucked the end of his biro thoughtfully: 'And it looks as though they knew their way around your house. Did any of the local kids know you were going away?'

Richard's heart sank as he began to put two and two together, remembering how he had happily chatted to the club boys about Wales and the mini-railway into Barmouth from the holiday cottage.

As the club resumed the following week, one particular group of children were noticeable because of their absence... including a very slim athletic young lad. Two and two make...

At our Ministry Support Team meeting we discussed the burglary. 'Of course, people get their houses ransacked all the time,' said one member thinking he was being helpful. 'It's just one of those things.'

Mary C. spoke up: 'But I feel this is very different. I think it was one of the children we were trying to help, so I feel let down. It wasn't my fault at all, but it happened to me because I'm here, on the Lord's work. And it's as if the kids just walked all over me.'

* * *

Fortunately, Mary and Richard are empowered: able to deal with situations and to work them through. But many of the folk we seek to minister to are far removed from such basic abilities. The new and developing culture of the third millennium ensures an excellent lifestyle for those with power and possibilities. The 'yuppies' on television display how life ought to be: full of dynamic fast living, good cars, good money, good looks, good holidays, good jobs, good sex, good lifestyle... success breeding success!

Yet ministry on today's outer estates means living alongside many of the disempowered of this new society: the 'hidden poor', those who haven't made it. The teenage mothers for whom the great promise of single-parent life has turned into brokenness; the folk set in the poverty trap who can never hope to achieve the normal lifestyle displayed so wonderfully on the television; the youths who are stunted – often physically as well as mentally – because of the continued cycle of deprivation. Then there are the old-age pensioners who are also disempowered because they are terrified of becoming victims; the people who are supposed to be receiving care in the community; the long-term disabled; the inadequate.

Many outer estates are becoming ghettos for the helpless and hopeless. Little wonder that anger seethes almost physically; youths roam the streets and occasionally riot; old-age pensioners become prisoners in their own homes; criminality becomes acceptable; children 'joy ride'; fathers fail to take responsibility; swearing and violence are normal. Apathy caused by powerlessness grips the community, and in the midst of this confused society live thousands of people who keep themselves to themselves and have little clue as to what is going on around them.

People are discovering that the ground of life has shifted radically, and there is no going back. We are at the end, so I am told, of the Enlightenment or modernist culture that has pervaded the West since the time of Darwin. Instead of learning 'timeless' values, our children are drifting aimlessly in the fast new world of computer-friendly soundbites.

Bishop Michael Whinney writes helpfully:

> There are disorientating mists swirling all around us today. Values are changing: 'Everything is relative'. We are told, 'No more moral absolutes'. The givenness of God's truths is judged and found wanting. Habits are changing: consumerism rules – OK? (*Birmingham Diocesan Bulletin 1996*)

And Graham Cray, Principal of Ridley Hall Theological College, comments:

Our gleaming shopping malls are our new Cathedrals – as we know, worship takes place there every day including Sundays. 'Tesco ergo sum', being freely translated as 'I shop therefore I am'. The era is changing; we are Post-Enlightemnent, Post-Modernist, Post-Christian... we are surfing the net – but to where? (*Anglican Renewal Conference 1998*)

Outer estates are the raw and open wound of this new culture – the 'poor and needy' of the postmodern society. I reiterate again how desperately we need empowered Christians who are willing to give up their comfortable and often successful lifestyles to be missionaries to the disempowered who are the 'hidden poor' of our society.

At the same time as our 'scaffolding' team were discovering the pain of living at this raw end of the new culture, their outer-estate church was showing more signs of life. But the devil is rarely happy to see the things of God progressing, and this became obvious as personal opposition escalated...

12

Telephones, Taxis and Fire!

Suffering produces perseverance; perseverance, character and character, hope.

Romans 5:3

'Am I glad to see you!' exclaimed Jeremy as we returned from an evening meeting. He looked quite white, and behind him our other children stood with relief written all over their faces. 'Crazy Carl's been here again,' declared Nick in a worried tone.

My heart skipped a beat. Carl had taken to the vicarage, becoming a regular visitor – generally at about 11 p.m. In the early days, I'd opened the door and tried to reason with him. But his whole body language was so utterly violent that I'd begun to speak to him from the upstairs bathroom window. He would regale me with obscenities and incoherent shouting until he got fed up or the police arrived.

Nick started the story by picking up the building brick lying beside the front step. 'He's been hammering on the door with this!' he exclaimed angrily. 'And on the window! I've no idea why it didn't break. And he was shouting at us through the letterbox.'

Elizabeth joined in: 'Mum, it was awful. I thought he was going to get in and attack us. I didn't know what was happening.'

Just then a siren rent the air, and a police car screeched to a halt outside. Two officers approached the front door, wondering about the little group gathered there. They were responding, rather belatedly, to our children's 999 call.

I turned to one of the officers whom I knew. 'It's Carl again. It looks as if he's gone now, but he's been threatening my family with that brick.' They knew who Carl was, right enough. Everybody knew Carl: 6ft 6ins, with shoulders almost as broad, dressed like a middle-aged skinhead complete with 'bovver' boots. Over his left knuckles was tattooed the word 'love'. Not particularly appropriate in his case. He invariably reeked of drink, his speech was mostly unintelligible and altogether he was a very fearsome person.

Sometime later. Carl disappeared from the scene. I guessed he'd been rehoused because I knew the neighbours were anxious to move him on. However, I later learned he had been jailed for ten years. convicted of buggery and firearms offences.

Mary and I have often thought back to that terrifying night when Carl accosted our children. Did he have a gun in his pocket then? Was it the grace of God that saved us yet again from 'Murder at the Vicarage'? Ministry is not as simple or as removed from the real world as many people would suggest. It costs to live in a vicarage in the midst of such a difficult area. And the battle is ongoing – that's the hardest part. Just when l felt I'd broken through, so the darkness descended again. I've found that being a missionary for the kingdom of God is hard, unremitting, grinding work.

* * *

'Wallace?' Mary whispered across the bed. 'Wallace? It's ringing again!'

'Oh no!' I thought to myself. 'Not again.' I wasn't so concerned about the telephone ringing at 1 am., but about the effect it would have on Mary. I knew that her heart would be palpitating wildly, ending all hope of sleep, and that when I answered the telephone, no one would reply – not even with abuse. It would happen repeatedly.

'Why don't you just disconnect the telephone?' some kindly person asked as we shared our problem with our Ministry Support Team. 'Or even change the number?'

'It isn't as simple as that,' Mary replied patiently. 'It's not so much the actual call itself, but the intrusion into our house and family. Even if we disconnect it every night, somebody out there will still be "doing it". Don't you see?'

Actually I didn't see fully. It seemed to me that if the phone lead was pulled out, that would be the end of it.

'I can see exactly what Mary means,' said Julie Thompson. 'You men! You're so insensitive!' Did she mean all men in general or me in particular? I suspected the latter.

'Yes,' said Janet. 'Whoever it is is still thinking the thoughts and wanting to upset you. It's not as if it's a random call. I think it's because you're at the vicarage.'

After some discussion, we took the wise advice of the team and had a private ex-directory line installed. We were able, to a limited degree, to separate church affairs from our private lives, but I found it so hard that I had given myself to the area and was having it thrown back in my face.

That wasn't the end of the story though. Shortly afterwards, instead of the telephone ringing, the front door bell shrilled. The first call was at 2.30 a.m., and we both shot up in bed, totally awake. Was it Carl, much later than normal and probably more drunk? Or was it...?

I hung out of the bathroom window. I could see the top of a man's head. What could he possibly want at this time of night?

'What is it?' I asked him in a none-too-pleasant tone.

His head shot round and looked up. 'Your taxi for the airport.' He looked expectantly at me. And, yes, outside on the road I saw his taxi standing ready.

'No, there must be some mistake,' I replied innocently. I felt better and cooler. Probably just a computer error or something like that. He merely shrugged his shoulders and made some remark about 'those b*** kids' again.

'It's OK, dear,' I said to Mary. 'Just a taxi with a wrong address.' We decided together it could be a mistake, turned over and went back to sleep.

The front door bell shrilled again at 3.30 a.m. 'Don't tell me, taxi for the airport?' I said as I leaned out of the window. This was bad. I couldn't explain this away to Mary. Somebody was doing this on purpose.

The bell went again at 4.30 a.m. I knew what it would be. And I was right. 'Mary, I'm going to disconnect that bell and put a note on the door.'

We have not ordered a taxi or pizza or anything. Trouble with hoax calls

The note went on the Vicarage door at bedtime for many weeks, greatly adding to our sense of vulnerability and 'being got at'. Several times I heard footsteps up the pathway... and then back down again after the note had been read. I began to understand for the first time Mary's comment about the intrusion she felt. Further, was the whole thing a deliberate ploy by someone with a grudge? Was the enemy involved in aiding and abetting? I felt out of my depth and depression loomed.

Mary and I prayed often about our fears. We harassed the Lord, just as the Bible tells us to. We asked the Ministry Support Team to lay hands on us. But in the middle of the night I felt so alone. It was my responsibility to protect my family, and yet helplessness hung over me. I wouldn't discuss the problem with Mary as I felt it would upset her. It was easy to withdraw irritably as an obtuse way of getting my own back on life in general and God in particular! However, God took no notice of my little demonstration and the heavens seemed grey and lifeless. Was God testing us again? Was I just a hopeless husband / father / pastor / priest / Christian? Was I a failure without enough faith? The questions surged, but answers were few.

It's hard to be a Christian leader, because so many of us feel that others would have coped in many situations and even come out smiling Also, we tend to retreat into ourselves and become 'beaming' wrecks. Challenge Christians who put on a brave face in the midst of adversity and you'll find they'll mostly be living a lie, escaping into separateness as a false protection of their faith. Leaders living in challenging areas need to stand up against the lie of being a failure!

Another trial awaited us...

* * *

'It's nothing to worry about now,' said the dancing instructor as he stood on the vicarage doorstep. 'We've managed to put it out. So it's all sorted for the moment.'

He continued, 'But we were worried when we saw the curtain going up in flames. Do you know what they did?'

Conal leaned forward as he spoke: 'The idiots smashed a hole in that glass door and then dragged the end of the curtain through.' He looked incredulous and then exclaimed. 'And they just set light to it... for no reason at all! The whole thing was ablaze in next to no time. Right into the hall!'

His concern showed clearly as he explained: 'I was so worried because we were having a party and the little girls were all dressed up in their frilly frocks. They could easily have caught fire. I dread to think what could have happened because the whole wall's scorched, though we caught it straight away.'

Afterwards I angrily remarked to our churchwardens, 'I'll bet it was that group we caught jumping off the roof last week. They've been hanging around. We were lucky this time. Both the children and the church are all right, but it was a near thing.'

David agreed. 'And if the dance class hadn't been there, well, the whole lot would have gone up in no time. What a mess it would have been. Just from a few vandals and a box of matches.'

Mary was more to the point: 'But what if they do it to the vicarage? When we are asleep at night? It would just burn up, wouldn't it? Even with all the smoke alarms.'

Her comments proved not totally unfounded because during the next week we saw smoke rising from the bottom of our garden.

'Dad! Dad, the fence is on fire,' shouted Nicholas from a viewpoint in his bedroom. 'I'll ring the fire brigade.'

After the remains of the fence had been well soaked it was discovered that fuel had been deliberately piled up against the wooden palings.

Of course, Mary was deeply distraught: 'First the telephone, then the taxis, and now fire. Wallace, I don't know if I can cope with any more of this. And look at the hole in the fence. The dogs can get out and they can all get in! What are you going to do about it?'

I couldn't think of anything to do. Of course we prayed. But we are part of this world and cannot expect some sort of godly passport to a trouble free existence. As Jesus says in the Sermon on the Mount, 'He causes his sun to rise on the evil and the good, and sends rain on the righteous and the unrighteous.' (*Matthew 5:45*) Incarnational ministry in troublesome areas is arduously and continually demanding. Everything seems to be against you.

The problems didn't even end there Some local youths broke a window in our caravan on the vicarage driveway and threw a firework into it. The van burst into flames. Our Nicholas threw open the door and retrieved the gas cylinder as the flames grew higher. What would have happened to him if it had exploded? The caravan was a write-off. We had no insurance. And no way of spending a quiet night away from the estate. I felt trapped.

How exhausting it all is – not just for the vicarage family, but for all who are on the battlefield against the enemy. This should come as no surprise to the biblical Christian, who will remember how Christ himself was an innocent victim, even to death on the cross. And how eleven of the twelve disciples met with some sort of violent death because of their association with the Son of God. Even John was exiled for his faith. We thank God for our Ministry Support Team, who stood by us right through the darkest times. In our better moments we even thank God for putting us in the raw and open wound of the new culture within our postmodern estate.

Despite this personal battle. and possibly because of it, authentic spiritual life was slowly creeping into the church itself, even if the cost was high for the 'scaffolding'. There was also a perception of slowly dawning excitement as a trickle of people met with Christ. Paul instructs us to 'rejoice in our sufferings, because we know that suffering produces perseverance; perseverance, character; and character, hope.' (*Romans 5:3*) Even when feeling really down, I could sense that Paul was quite right. The problems we were enduring could end our ministry, or they could be character building, as they were for the apostle. So I could vaguely begin to praise God in it all. There was hope, and hope does not disappoint us.

Yet it all felt so weak and tentative. When I spoke to other leaders, their fellowships always seemed so thriving and strong. I questioned, 'Am I truly following God? Why do other leaders have so few difficulties?' I was continuing to learn about 'church speak'. Many churches pretend the problems don't exist, rather than learning to deal with them.

13

'He Sets Fire to Things, You Know'

The God of all grace... will himself restore you and make you strong, firm and streadfast.

1 Peter 5:10

What a day! What a week! What a job! Nothing had gone right. I was on the minister's roller coaster. How is it possible to cope with a life swinging from exciting highs to terrible lows all in the space of a week? Even sometimes from one hour to the next? Ups and downs are part of the battle, and I was right at the bottom. At least for the moment...

The previous night's PCC meeting had not gone well, punctuated as it was by fearful sounds of smashing glass and whooping kids. Terry had angrily fingered the offending stone; other more practical folk had gone in search of the well-used dustpan and brush. Glass-breaking was the current 'in thing' and the church was very vulnerable.

'Why should I bother if the parents don't?' I was thinking, as exasperation at senseless damage welled up to a point of near explosion, when suddenly a new voice came from behind.

'Excuse me, Father. But could you be helping me?'

I spun round to meet a shabbily dressed Irishman, with an anxious, subservient expression on his partly shaven face.

'It's like this. Father,' he went on. oblivious to the fact that I was clearly in the middle of other matters. My council looked on in muted amusement.

'It's like this,' he repeated. 'My father's dying and I need to be with him. I'm sorry to trouble you, sir, but I can't get home, you see. It's the bus fare He's in Liverpool, like.'

His face was troubled, he looked needy and I felt utterly trapped. Yet I sensed he was skilfully luring me into parting with money.

The sound of Terry boarding up the window reverberated as I groaned to myself, 'One thing at a time... please!' I crept back home seeking escape.

Mary greeted me: 'That radio's been on full blast again tonight. Do you know, the noise in the garden hit me like a solid wall. That's every night this week so far. I don't know why we're here in the first place! Do you? God said to us, "Settle down and plant gardens." Well, how can I with all that racket going on out the back? Talk about nearer to God in a garden; it's nearer to bedlam out there!'

The telephone rang.

'Can you tell me what to do about getting married at your church?' said the breathless feminine voice.

'At 11 o'clock at night? You've got to be joking!' I snapped irritably, almost slamming the telephone down.

'Are the angels asleep?' I pondered irreverently, as we lay down for another sleepless night. All was far from well at the vicarage!

∗ ∗ ∗

Life, for me at least, was a series of highs and lows. Rather like the wave pattern of an oscilloscope. On the one hand, I was beginning to see some dynamic fruit of ministry as God showed his supernatural power coupled with exciting faith risks. And, of course, the wonderful arrival of Martin and Janet Knox, followed by Elizabeth's dream, enabled us to create a Ministry Support Team to lead the church forward. Furthermore, the smallish, steady growth in both the health and size of our fellowship, though tenuous. was very real. Yet at the same time. the sheer physical effort of living on an outer estate sapped my vitality. I could almost feel the 'soggy blanket' of spiritual darkness that enveloped the area, shrouding us in apathy and a sense of hopelessness.

Furthermore, the continual demands of the new, and as yet untaught, Christians necessitated a needs-driven ministry.

The church itself was in a state of flux as the presence of the Holy Spirit became more apparent: seekers who arrived unexpectedly in church on some sort of 'spiritual wave' induced exciting, exhausting demands; new Christians needed profound support because of their rapidly changing lifestyle; some traditional church members portrayed seemingly selfish agendas; needy people without food, or in the middle of traumatic personal crisis, clamoured for assistance. And it was all happening within the context of our stressful living conditions.

Certainly something beautiful was happening. I knew that. But I was so bewildered by intense personal needs, and becoming desperately tired. Yet God had more for us.

One Sunday morning a new family started coming to church: Tom, Jean and their five children. A normal nuclear unit, it seemed, except... well, first of all, the children smelt. Church members quickly noticed their matted, greasy hair. And the kids would literally fling themselves onto any lap – offered or not! Unfortunately their smell preceded them. With no understanding that sometimes people need to meet quietly with God the children ran riot. The parents thought it quite normal. Perhaps it was to them.

The Sunday school helpers feared the arrival of these kids; especially young Kurt, who would stand on a table and scream and scream incessantly. This child obviously wanted attention, and his ploy succeeded very well indeed. Some mothers kept their own children well clear, perhaps rightly concerned about any peer relationships that might develop. Or were they simply worried about nits?

The new family had a profound impact, yet they were only symptomatic of our growing pains as a Christian fellowship. True, they were desperately needy of both God's love and church help. But then so were many others. The spiritual dynamic of the church was in danger of being clogged up by need. So what was to be done?

There are two ways forward when situations become overwhelming. One is to work out the pragmatic solution. This, unfortunately, is the normal way of so many churches. Often God has led and grown the church only for leaders to fall back on their own abilities and answers. The 'Red Sea' of faith possibilities becomes a wilderness and God's people are left walking in circles.

The second and right way is to seek God. The Ministry Support Team were left in no doubt as to his answer. We were to take as many folk as possible to one of the large Christian summer camps. On the face of it, this seemed a ridiculous way forward: creating more and more work for the more able, especially my support team. But God was adamant. Reasons became clear as we thought and prayed about the concept of 'tenting out' about 70 people for a week. On the social side, many of them had never been on any sort of holiday – some children had never even seen a cow. But God showed us even more important issues: the need for an 'external' faith environment to reinforce our teaching on spiritual realities: the necessity of seeing God at work in a tangible arena; the importance of creating space in a prayerful environment where basic problems behind personal needs can be exposed and radically dealt with. All these things added up to the development of a new dynamic of spirituality within the church, so helping our disparate membership to become a real Christian community.

The very next week I found myself keeping an appointment with a probation officer and social worker. Our new family, it seemed, were very well known.

'Yes,' I replied to their incredulous question. 'We are thinking of taking that whole family to camp. I mean, the kids have never been away from the estate, so it seems a great idea.'

'Well, if you're sure…' said one of them rather slowly. 'The little boy's very difficult. He sets fire to things, you know.'

* * *

Tom and Jean arrived for the camp with absolutely nothing. No bedding, no change of clothes, no food, no money – nothing, except what they stood in. as if they were simply out for a walk and happened to pass by the church. They stood around without a care in the world as their children wreaked havoc on the neatly piled equipment.

On the Monday night, Tom and Jean went to the main tent meeting. In fact they wandered off as if their new baby and toddlers didn't exist.

'Whatever are we going to do with that pair?' remarked Maureen, echoing worries about their irresponsible attitude.

The meeting progressed; Tom and Jean stood up as the speaker made his invitation. Then, almost immediately, they both fell in the Spirit, laid out completely in front of everybody.

'How's this happening?' questioned one of our stalwart helpers indignantly. 'I mean, they're not even Christians, are they? It's not fair. It's never happened to me!'

But others were smiling. This was what we'd hoped would happen. It was the basic reason for all the hassle, expenditure and work of bringing them to camp. Tom and Jean were meeting with Jesus Christ. It was wonderful.

I was sitting in my awning when they returned. They walked purposelessly around, fish and chips in their hands. How had they procured them with no money? They didn't even glance at their tent. How did they know their children were safe? Did they really care? As we relaxed with our bedtime drink, we wondered about the consequences of the evening.

The following morning, a young woman called Kim dashed up to our caravan. Her eyes were sparkling and she had a huge grin on her face. 'Do you know what happened last night after everyone had gone to bed?' The words tumbled out. 'We saw some angels! They really were angels! So big they were, and bright and beautiful. You ask the others if you don't believe me. And do you know, they were singing and it was lovely. Oh! I feel so good!'

She certainly looked good, and full of the Lord. Her excitement was infectious. Now I've never seen angels personally, although I've definitely seen their effect within physical situations. But Kim was bouncing with certainty.

Afterwards Mary said, 'Do you remember when Kim first came to St B's? Hasn't she changed since then? She's a different person. And I think she probably did see angels. After all, why not? They have a sound biblical basis.'

I was too busy remembering back to Kim's first visit to St B's. She'd gone to buy her *News of the World* one Sunday morning, saw the church doors open and 'knew' she had to enter – just as the service was beginning. She was dressed in motorbike leathers and carrying a crash helmet. Two days later she unexpectedly turned up at Praise and Prayer. Even with her leathers off, she looked rather wild and slightly unmanageable.

'I'm known as "the Joker"', she'd told us painfully. 'I've always got to make people laugh. But it isn't the real me. Even when I get the laughs I'm so sick of myself.' She hesitated. 'You see, nobody knows how I truly feel. Deep inside. Because I'm just "the Joker"'.

Later, after she'd listened with rapt attention to simple testimonies about spiritual reality, she interrupted dramatically, 'This knowing Jesus you're all talking about. I want it! Now!' It was as if God had grabbed hold of Kim almost bodily, then hurled her into the kingdom.

For some of the children, the camp was their very first holiday. Gemma was so pleased to be there; in her seven-year-old eyes it was absolutely fantastic. She was amazed that everyone was so nice and she walked around with a massive smile all week. Her mum, Judy, had a traumatic background. She was only a child herself. Her several boyfriends vied with each other for 'favours', and she'd moved from house to flat to maisonette, hoping to escape loan sharks and irate suitors. Judy liked to spend time on her own, wandering around the camp. She told Maureen about her experience later that week: 'It was lovely. I wandered into the empty meeting tent and heard a sort of voice saying, "Judy. Come over here." I somehow knew it was Jesus; and then I saw him, holding out his arms. I didn't really want to go. I was frightened. But I knew I had to, so I walked across the tent and I could see him there, beckoning. When I got to him, he reached out his hand and touched me. Then he was gone.

'Oh, Maureen,' she continued. 'It was so real. Not at all like a dream. It really happened.' Judy, like her daughter, passed the rest of the week with her whole face lit up.

Doug was a big man. A man's man. He was tall and broad and rugged-looking – not to be messed with. Sometime before the camp, he'd been invited to a national Christian celebration, and found it a very positive experience, if somewhat confusing.

'I never thought religion would be like that,' he remarked to his mate who took him along. 'It's not for a load of namby-pamby wimps, is it? And the music is all right!' He shook his head as if surprised at himself. 'I reckon there must be something in this Jesus business. I felt different – know what I mean?'

Terry, who was equal in size to Doug, turned to him and agreed: 'That's what I've found. It's real. Not just a load of hypocrites like I always thought religion was all about.'

A few months later in the local pub. Terry said, 'How's about you and Sadie coming to the camp with us? It'd be great, wouldn't it?'

'Camp? What do you mean?' replied Doug, as the remainder of the pint slid easily down his throat.

'Set 'em up again and I'll tell you,' countered Terry. 'It's your round anyway.'

Terry explained about the Christian camp. 'And you've never experienced anything like it, mate. Four thousand Christians together – the power is just amazing. Mind you,' he went on with a twinkle in his eye, 'you know that you and Sadie can't sleep in the tent together! It wouldn't be right, would it? Not in a Christian camp like.'

'What do you mean?' questioned Doug.

'Well, you're not married, are you?' Terry ribbed him. 'You're living in sin, aren't you? That's what you and Sadie are doing. It's not so bad in your own house, but in the camp? It wouldn't be right there.'

Doug arrived at the camp with Sadie in tow; separate bedrooms without even a murmur. Would he go to any of the meetings? He always seemed to have a good excuse for not doing so. But on the Friday night, I saw him stand up, go forward and commit his life to Jesus Christ as Lord and Saviour. How we all rejoiced. Doug had become a Christian. What a wonderful end to a wonderful week.

The consequence of the camp in the life of the church was amazing. After arriving home I went out the following morning to lead worship in the church. I felt as though I were dancing on clouds because I was so acutely aware of God's active presence. The whole of the group of 70 had returned with a different attitude to the Lord and his church. There was a freshness and vitality pervading the worship and a new dimension of faith that broke the continual cycle of apathy, disappointment and even despair. And even though I was now doubly exhausted, I felt strong and ready.

Christian leaders can expect exhaustion. I'm quite certain that at times Jesus must have been totally worn out, physically and emotionally. It's part of the cost of our calling. But the weariness of despair and the tiredness of hard work are two different matters. God's way forward, for me, broke the cycle of ups and downs that sheer weariness often brings. Peter put it more clearly when he said, 'The God of all grace... will himself restore you and make you strong, firm and steadfast.' (*1 Peter 5:10*)

As time went by we began to see some of the long-term effect on individuals. For Tom and Jean one tangible result was yet another baby! And their little boy stopped 'setting fire to things.'

Kim went from strength to strength, glowing in the Lord and continually seeking to live rightly for him. When she gave her personal testimony, it was great to see 'the Joker' share profound truths about Almighty God her Saviour and Lord. Today. Kim is the co-leader of a small Christian conference centre.

Judy has gone back to her live-in boyfriend, and back to her former lifestyle miles away from our church. Even after her wonderful spiritual experience the 'flesh' was just too much. So l have to leave her to the Lord and pray that one day she will return to him. However, I have heard that Gemma, her daughter, still attends a church.

Terry and Doug meander on through life. Often Doug will go months without coming near church and then suddenly he is one of our keenest members for a short time. Terry plugs away working with the disabled and rarely misses a Sunday.

Mary often says to me in moments of exasperation, 'Wallace, I can't understand God. I mean, why doesn't he bring them all through to a deep faith and commitment?'

It's apparent that Tom, Jean, Judy, Kim, Doug and Terry have reacted to God's love in very different ways. Free will is certainly part of the reason, together with the personality makeup of our genetic inheritance. However, home background and environment play a very important part. Indeed, the sociological backdrop is paramount in our thinking about such things.

We have always noticed that the three estates of our parish look quite reasonable. The housing stock, on the whole, is not unpleasant. We have seven high-rise blocks of flats, but even those are not a terrible eyesore. And the vast majority of our housing is fairly conventional, with front and back gardens, often along tree-lined roads. Indeed, when I first arrived, I wondered if I had been subconsciously drawn into a middle-class prejudice against council estates that was not based on reality. But the problems and needs are clearly manifest. So why do they arise? It doesn't make sense until we consider some quite unpleasant facts and statistics:

- In the UK, only 25 per cent of the adult population living in council housing receive their main income from employment. The remaining 75% receive their main income from benefits or pensions.

- Of the remaining 75 per cent, 12 per cent are lone parents. It is my experience that council accommodation is freely available to single (often teenage) mothers. (Or was, at the time of writing.) They tend to have under-developed social skills, and a sense of anti-authoritarianism prevails, with children often running wild on the streets. At one of our local primary schools, which is centred in an area with many 'lone parent' maisonettes, only two children who entered Year

3 are in the present Year 6 group. All the rest have moved on because of the mobility of their parent. The school has a yearly mobility of 60 per cent. and 80 percent receive free school meals.

- The unemployed equal 13 per cent. It is difficult for those who are unskilled to get employment that pays above poverty line benefits. Often people will find 'jobs on the side', which together with benefit will give an improved income. One man in my church, with five children, just cannot find work that will pay above minimum rates. So if he worked, his differential tax rate would be 94 per cent for every £1 earned! Not enough to pay for transport to work!

- The sick and disabled equal 10 per cent. Care in the community has meant a massive take up of council accommodation by some folk who are almost unable to cope, either physically or mentally. Unfortunately, the community structures are often at their weakest in the estates.

- Pensioners equal 40 per cent. In middle-class society, pensioners are a strong and effective lobby group. On the estates they tend to be marginalised by street gangs. Violence and verbal abuse have led to many pensioners becoming prisoners in their own homes outside school hours. They naturally become unprepared to take any effective role within the community. (*Figures derived from 'Families Resource Survey' DSS 1994, and from the 1991 census.*)

A few years ago, a lady vicar on a neighbouring estate who had reached her sixtieth birthday brought this home to me. She told me, 'Wallace, l never go out at night now. I close my curtains at 6 p.m. and that's it. Even if somebody knocks, or I hear noises outside. I won't budge. And all the older folk around here do exactly the same.' It has all become too much for her and she's recently retired to a more 'sane' area in the South West. The consequences of the sociological make-up of the estates are profound. Those who live there can no longer be called working class, either in an everyday sense of employment, or in the traditional 'salt of the earth' ethical understanding. Some sociologists would use the American term 'underclass' to best describe the majority of council-estate neighbourhoods. I prefer the term 'disempowered', because that's what many are.

The handful of 'empowered' residents tend to escape at weekends. The sprinkling of churchgoers from this group disappear to churches in areas that better reflect their status. The disempowered are stuck in the area because they have no transport and tend to be consumed by personal need and anxiety. It's difficult to turn the conversation to others, so they are far from natural leaders. Outer-estate churches tend to have very low numbers and very low possibilities. And the financial implications are obvious and problematic.

But back to Tom and Jean and the rest. My experience is clear. Even when people turn to Christ. and some have brilliant spiritual experiences, the battle has merely begun. The road to reflecting faith in lifestyle and personal holiness is extremely long, and time-consuming for the 'scaffolding'. It appears to take literally years to discard the disempowered lifestyle, so that people can become dynamic, able Christian disciples. And even then, there is another battle for their children in a community where values are definitively not Christian and the normal model is to shout, swear, blaspheme and over-use physical discipline.

Leaders who seek to emulate the way of Christ using only pragmatic convention and powerless formality, find the path impossibly long, arduous and painful. I see too many outer-estate churches working hard using 'reasonable' methods; their leaders lost in the despair of low attendance and overwhelming need. I know from personal experience the roller coaster of feelings that can decimate ministry in such areas.

Hearing God and acting upon his way forward, however obtuse it may seem to be, is the only way. Our church radically changed its spiritual dynamic by the simple expedient of a week together at a 'faith camp'.

14

'Tell the People... What Their Sins Are'

Tell the people... what their sins are.

Micah 3:8, GNB

I've always loved the market town of Ludlow. It seems to me to have that captivating combination of sleepiness and curiosity. The black-and-white buildings give a sense of timelessness; the bustling street-market a sense of vitality and life. So it was no great shock to our Ministry Support Team when I chose the town's Bishop Maskell Centre for our day away together.

'Well, surprise, surprise!' commented Martin. 'I suppose you're going to tell us that the venue is a word from God?'

I smiled because I felt safe. 'No, you're right. I just fancied it,' was my rejoinder.

We settled down in the comfortable chairs, but my mind was far from at ease. In fact I felt exasperated, especially with God. 'My' church wasn't growing quickly enough. It wasn't the centre of a new spiritual awakening yet. So I'd organised the 'away-day' to storm heaven and discover God's evangelistic plan. Organised missions have rarely (if ever) been successful in a council-estate setting. In fact one well-known tent evangelist 'sucked his tooth' and shook his head in our vicarage lounge as Mary and I even offered to underwrite the considerable expense.

'I don't think it'll work,' he'd said thoughtfully. 'You see, we really need small group meetings in people's homes as well as the big tent thing. But we've found house meetings don't fit in with the culture you've

111

described.' He added, 'Neither do the tent meetings, for that matter. It's really difficult to get things moving on the estates.'

Back in the sleepy comfort of the Ludlow centre, we quietly began our team meeting with a short study of the Scriptures. I particularly enjoy the intellectual stimulation of such sessions due to the diverse ways of thinking within the team. We can lightly argue and yet still be one in the Spirit.

But it was time to move on to listen to God. Over the years, I have adapted my own personal method to work within such a group. We will sit in companionable silence for quite a long period, with that wonderful sense of Jesus in our midst. Some will wander off to other parts of the building, but there is still a sense of Jesus encompassing the whole group as we each seek to hear God. When we come back together, I have always found a commonality of thinking: some people find that God gives them specific scriptures, others inspired thoughts, and still others have 'pictures' that God impresses on their minds. All in all, it's as if God shows us his truth for the situation, but from many different angles. And we suddenly see it all fits together like a gigantic jigsaw. Then once the godly principle is established we can move on to a team discussion of the practical outworking.

On this occasion one of the team started the comeback session with: 'I don't understand why. but the Lord has placed Micah 3:8 on my heart. Especially the bit where it says, "Tell the people... what their sins are".'

'That fits in so well with my thoughts,' said Janet. as she picked up the words of her husband. 'I was thinking of Isaiah 58:1. It says, "Shout it aloud... Declare to my people their rebellion and... their sins." It's the same sort of message, I think. Telling people about their sins. I wonder what it means?'

'Yes, I agree,' enthused Martin Thompson. His words were urgent: 'I believe the Lord is giving us a real message. Remember when Ezekiel was called to be a prophet? The Lord said to him, "I am sending you... to a... nation that has rebelled against me." (*Ezekiel 2:3*) That's how it is. That's the sin God wants us to point out.'

'What do you mean, Martin?' I asked tentatively. 'Are you saying that I've got to stand up and denounce adultery and all that sort of thing? I know I have to – that's one of the commandments – but how do you mean?' I was tripping over my own words, mostly because of a cold sense of fear creeping into my flesh. What did God expect of me?

'No, it's not like that, Wallace,' Martin replied. 'God's speaking to us about the same sin that Ezekiel and Isaiah pointed out. It's not so much the moral sins of life, like greed and so on. It's about attitude. The Hebrews were leaving God out of their lives and just living as they wanted to. They were rebelling by turning their backs on God.'

Janet took up the story: 'And once people leave God out of their lives and don't bother about him, morality and everything else goes out of the window. It all goes back to a right attitude to God, doesn't it?'

'That's it!' Maureen agreed excitedly. 'So God is telling us that the first sin is not taking any notice of him. That's what he finds so hurtful. Just like when the Hebrews rebelled against God and didn't really listen to what he said.'

'I think I'm beginning to see...' A glimmer of understanding was flickering in my mind. 'So you're not saying that God wants me to stand on street corners pointing the finger at people and shouting, "Turn from your sins, you adulterer!" It's all about godlessness in our society. That people have left God out of their lives, and that's really their greatest sin.'

Robert agreed: 'And it's going on all the time, all around us, as people, even children, ignore him. It's the sin that leads to all the others. Like our country: the more godless it becomes, the greater the moral decay. I'm sure that's what it all means.'

'Come on, let's leave it for an hour and go and have some lunch,' I said. It had been a good morning's work.

Mary and I meandered through the narrow streets of the market town. As we walked, the ideas of the morning would not leave my mind.

'Mary, what do I have to do?' I asked. My mind was whirling, and I felt the responsibility of leading whatever action was needed.

She smiled. 'We've already learned how Satan has a grip on the physical from the spiritual, haven't we? Well, God's shown us this morning that ordinary people turning their back on God brings darkness, just as we've already discovered Satan himself does. So it's all part of the same darkness. They both give the same result. Do you see?'

I answered, 'So God's taking us on a step further, and showing us where to concentrate our efforts? So his light can shine even more?'

'Yes,' she replied. 'His evangelistic plan, at this time, is for us to tell the people what their sins are. That they are somehow turning their backs on him. Snubbing him.'

We entered the coffee shop and I looked greedily at the choice of cream cakes.

* * *

One of the great problems of the Western church is that we are results orientated – evangelism can become merely a tool for bumping up numbers – whereas the call of true mission is to proclaim the gospel to people whether or not it is fashionable or even acceptable. That's not to say that we can communicate it in a culturally relevant way – such an approach is imperative. But above all, it is the word of God that needs proclaiming, and not our evangelistic strategy!

Ezekiel's call, as Martin had already pointed out, was to 'a rebellious nation'. But clearly he was not called to tickle the spiritual fancy of the moment. As it says in verse 7 of Ezekiel 2, 'You must speak my words to them, whether they listen or fail to listen, for they are rebellious.' It is enormously easy for the church to rebel in its mission strategy and offer the food people think they want, rather than the true bread of life. The church of God has a clear responsibility on its shoulders to proclaim truth; even if that truth does not, in the first instance, appear to bear fruit or grow membership. We are not to be a church that judges our message by its results.

'Telling people what their sins are' has since become the hallmark of St B's. Not in a self-righteous condemnatory way, but merely pointing people back to their loving heavenly Father and saying, 'The greatest sin is to ignore God; to make him an optional extra in your life. That really hurts him.' We've noticed that as people of all ages turn back to God, he starts to bring his light into their personal darkness. Take the example of Jim...

Jim arrived on the vicarage doorstep one September evening. He was carrying with him a confusing tale of woe.

'I've just been up the M5, along the hard shoulder.' he gasped out as I opened the door. 'I haven't got a car you see, so I had to walk. And it's been terrible since Margery last came out of hospital. Well, she hates it there, doesn't she? But then what else can they do? Last time, she went funny and ran screaming out of the house in her nightie. She was acting mad, she was. Gone four hours and only came back at half-past three in the morning. And she wouldn't say a word, so I hit her. I mean it wasn't right for her to do that, was it? But then I got to thinking they'd probably take her back to the hostel – you know, that one for battered wives. And I wished I hadn't hit her. And I know I shouldn't. But I can't help it. She's got bruises all over and there's the neighbours. The neighbours think we're terrible. Always shouting and screaming at each other. And I know the kids really hate me. Everybody thinks it's all my fault. But I can't seem to help it. I don't know what comes over me. And I did leave the note where they could see it, right under the telephone...'

'The note? What note?' My mind had been completely overwhelmed and I merely grabbed on to his last comment. 'You'd better come in and tell me about it.'

'I haven't got a car,' he repeated as I ushered him into the study.

I pushed out a chair. 'Sit down, Jim, and tell me about that note.'

'What do you mean? I've just told you, haven't I?' he exploded. In his clouded mind the story was utterly clear. 'I left the note by the telephone because I didn't want to worry them. And I just started walking. Miles it was. And I ended up on the M5 and it seemed a simple end to it all. But I couldn't do it, and suddenly I thought about the church, so here I am.'

I gulped. In the back of my mind I thought, 'Note? Suicide? Am I the alternative to suicide by juggernaut?' But then I thought, in a more positive frame of mind, 'Perhaps the Lord's bringing this man to me.'

Jim, however, was still in full flow: '... job going all to ruins because I'm never really there. Or if I am, my mind's all over the place, or I feel so depressed I just sit there, staring at the bench.' He hardly took time to draw breath. 'I think they want to sack me, but I need the money because I've got the loan sharks on my back, and the rent...' He stopped for a moment.

'Vicar, I'm a good father and husband, but nothing seems to work out properly. I don't know...' I could hear the doubt beginning to creep into his voice.

As the story went on, it seemed to me that suicide was a fair option. His whole life appeared to be one big disaster area. 'This man is right in the middle of the darkness,' I thought as Jim continued to talk and talk and talk. 'I'll have to tell him to stop turning his back on God.' The thought resounded in my mind. 'He'll have to stop living as if God doesn't exist.'

I interrupted, 'Jim, I want to tell you what God says about this. If you're such a good father and husband. why is your life such a mess? Why has your wife gone into that hostel? Why do your kids seem to hate you? Why does your boss want to get rid of you? It doesn't make sense. does it?'

Jim told me afterwards that this comment had proved to be a turning point. I was the first one who had ever spoken to him, man to man, and not merely glossed over his faults to make him feel good about himself. He told me that he had spoken to people at the day centre, his doctor and everybody else, but they had just kept talking about his father and where he was brought up, saying, 'It isn't really your fault, Jim.' But he knew it was. At least a lot of it was. So he hadn't seen the point in listening to them.

After my unexpected interruption, Jim leaned forward. I could see the grief and pain in his eyes. 'So what can I do about it? What can I do about me? I can't help being like I am. Is it possible for a man to change?'

'Jim, the only way is to ask God into your life. It's as straightforward as that.' A thought struck me so I added, 'All your life you've known that God created you; that God is God. But you've never cared tuppence about him. It's as if he didn't exist for you. You've been your number one. And look where it's got you.'

He nodded in agreement. It was making sense. Yes, he had always known that God was God, but didn't want to bother with him. So he'd carried on regardless. He thought he knew better than his Maker.

Jim looked chastened. 'I know what you mean. Because even when I was on the motorway this morning, I seemed to have a voice in my head telling me it was all wrong. And this time I took notice of it and came to see you. But other times, I've said, "Oh, to hell with it!" Do you think that's been God speaking to me, Vicar?'

That same night, two hours after Jim knocked on the vicarage door I had the wonderful privilege of leading him to the Lord. Today, Jim is a mature Christian and church leader. His wife Margery has come to faith herself and has lost all need for hospital assistance. She is becoming a stable and mature person in her own right. Together, they are part of God's light shining out into the darkness, even bringing their neighbours to church. They have been truly saved.

Jim takes us back to God's heart. It is on God's heart that he wants 'all men to be saved and to come to a knowledge of the truth.' (*1 Timothy 2:4*) His Spirit often brings people to a point of crisis, just as Jesus himself did as he ministered on the shores of Galilee. Surely the church has to be ready to work in accord with the Spirit of God; using crises in people's lives to bring about God's purposes, while being lovingly careful not to take advantage of their predicament. Jim was right in thinking that God had spoken to him on the motorway, in the midst of his anguish. However, he needed a human agency to break through his other false thoughts. Ministers (lay or ordained) need to hear God for individual people, otherwise we spend our whole lives probing cul-de-sacs rather than speaking out God's message.

People like Jim remind me of a great hole in the ecclesiastical system. Obviously some people have to be gently nurtured into the kingdom. It's a case of coming alongside and leading them tenderly to the Saviour. But for many others, confrontation is totally necessary to jerk them out of themselves so that they can see the whole picture. So how does one know which approach to use? The system would certainly indicate the former: straightforward pastoral care and loving concern. Yet how often such an approach leaves people, in the words of John Wesley, 'almost Christians'. Sentimentally vague and biblically uninformed – hardly the stuff that brings men to become cross-centred Christians! As Jesus himself clearly stated, 'You will know the truth, and the truth will set you free.' (*John 8:32*)

Leading people to faith is wonderful. But our growing church had to learn to cope with the converts: people with very diverse needs and problems.

15

Wild Grapes

*What more could I have done? Why did my vineyard give me wild grapes
instead of sweet?*

Isaiah 5:4, TLB

'Vicar, that was a lovely service,' smiled Georgina as we shook hands. I
preened myself and then replied, 'That's great. Which of my three points
did you find particularly helpful?'

She looked slightly bewildered. 'Oh, I didn't mean your sermon. I was
talking about the worship. That group of songs and the silence
afterwards was just right.' She added, 'Of course your talk was nice as
well. It was everything together, you see.'

Georgina was quite right. The worship of the church had become
particularly good. Adrian, a specialist on drums as well as keyboard and
piano, had just moved into the area. His sensitive contribution in our
growing band added a vibrant backing to our worship songs. But more
important than the music was a growing sense of true worship
emanating from the hearts of the congregation. And the church was still
growing, not with people from far and wide, but with folk from the area
who had responded to the gospel and met with the Lord.

Richard Flowerday looked at his watch. 'Wallace, we'll never make a
good Anglican of you. That service lasted an hour and three-quarters,
and look, nobody wants to leave.'

Sure enough almost the whole congregation were standing around
talking and drinking coffee. The sense of true Christian fellowship

created a lovely atmosphere. And I felt good, even if very tired. It was worth all the past hassle to see God building his church.

That same Sunday night, I glowed as I sat with the Ministry Support Team. I slowly noticed, however, that no one shared my satisfaction. Janet looked weary; Maureen sighed – loudly; Martin and Julie Thompson were obviously down; even Martin Knox was jaded.

I said, 'Come on, you lot! You're letting Old Nick get at you. Things are really good. Just open your eyes!'

There's nothing worse than having somebody full of the joys of spring when others feel heavy and tired.

Mary Chamberlain responded first: 'Look, Wallace, I agree that the church is going well. But it's on our backs. I feel shattered, and look around you: everyone's exhausted.'

My wife joined in. 'Yes, I agree. There are so many people now, with so many needs. And each one sucks us dry of emotion and care. I feel worn out too, Mary.'

Julie stirred herself into life and commented, 'Take us, for instance. Dave and Karen have been almost living at our house for weeks now, and we're drained. But what else can we do? We can't just shrug them off.'

She reminded us of the story. This brother and sister had been thrown out of the family home on the other side of Birmingham. The mother's new live-in boyfriend didn't want them cluttering up the place, so she'd half-arranged for them to go and live with her sister on our estate while things cooled down… or until she got fed up with the new man.

Unfortunately, Auntie wasn't very excited about the visit of Dave and Karen, so during an argument she pushed them out of the front door. Then, cursing and shouting, she showered their few possessions from the bedroom window. The neighbours were most interested, especially the local youths who came and 'helped' the situation by jeering cynically at everyone.

Martin Thompson took up the story: 'And next morning I met them in the Valley during my jogging practice. They were in a dreadful mess. They'd obviously slept rough that night, and were emotionally distraught. So I brought them home for some breakfast. And Auntie didn't really want them back at all, so they've been practically living with us for three weeks now.'

'It's just too much,' responded Julie. 'I mean, I love to help, but it's as Mary says, I'm exhausted.'

Janet joined in: 'And look what's happened to us! Did you know that Norma was round our house again the other day?' Norma was a recently converted Christian, who hadn't quite got the idea of how it all worked. 'She said to me, "Doesn't the Bible say that all Christians should share what they have with each other? Well, Janet, I need a car. I mean, if you give me a car, I'll be able to take the kids to school and then go off to work properly. You and Martin have two, so why don't you give me one?" What on earth do you say to that? And I felt guilty because I had to say no. Even if I had given her one, she wouldn't have been able to afford to run it. She'd probably have sold it and bought something stupid with the money.'

Mary C. eagerly agreed. 'And I've had Billie and her four children staying with Richard and me in our two-bedroomed house. I really love her, and it's a joy to serve her, but I'm so tired and I never seem to get a moment to myself.'

Even Martin Knox stepped into the fray. 'I've not stopped helping first the Turners and then the Johnsons with all their financial problems. And with Daphne's possible marriage break-up on the horizon, it seems to go on for ever.'

I began to realise why they all looked so down in the mouth. It wasn't that things weren't going well. In fact in many ways they were going too well as need after need was flooding into the life of the church. The team were clearly telling me the overload light had turned to a dangerous red.

Maureen continued: 'And I've just been round to Teri's house. You've never seen anything like it. The dirt is appalling. They've got no furniture and the kitchen's from another planet; just full of dirty dishes and pans and nappies. Then Teri said to me, "What can I do?" I nearly caught myself replying, "Why don't you start with soap and water?" But I knew the answer wasn't that simple. Nobody seems to know how to help themselves. They just drain us instead.' She looked over at me, as if for an answer; so I continued to sink deeper into my chair and make meaningful signs to Martin about coffee and biscuits. When at last he suggested a break for drinks, I shot up and said, 'Come on, I'll help you.' And under my breath I added, 'Let this lot stew in their own discouragement.' The reader will note that 1 am full of care and compassion for all!

During coffee, my wife asked the sensible question: 'What is the Lord saying to us through all this? On one side the church is doing really well. But here we are, exhausted by physical, mental and spiritual stress. What does it all mean?' Then she began to answer her own question: 'I suppose it's this incarnational ministry thing again. It's the cost of serving – especially in such a needy area.'

Martin Thompson took up the flow: 'Yes, it's not about where we would feel comfortable or about our natural ministry or natural environment. After all, earth itself was hardly Jesus' natural environment. None of us would have chosen to come and live here, would we? But we are here because God has called us, and that's great, isn't it?'

* * *

I went alone to the convent. I knew I needed to seek God's will and purposes for the way out of our extreme exhaustion. Over the past months, I had learned to further develop a kind of contemplative listening to God, where he spoke even more deeply through a sort of 'knowledge' at the centre of my being.

I sat in the retreat room and formed my thoughts into questions: 'Lord, why are my Ministry Support Team exhausted? Why are there so many people with so many problems overwhelming our slender resources? Why does everything rest on a few? Why aren't all our new converts "hot" for Jesus? Why is it that some have wonderful spiritual experiences and then seem to fall to pieces the following week? Why won't they willingly throw themselves into faith matters? Why don't they show wonderful spiritual fruit? Why won't they take responsibility for themselves? Why is it that folk who have entered into leadership somehow fall at the first hurdle as if they were baby Christians, and expect us to pick up the pieces? *Why is it all so lukewarm?* Is it a symptom of many years of disempowerment, or mere carelessness and lack of application? Perhaps it's a general malaise that affects many churches, regardless of the social background.'

The answer came speedily and was not, to my mind, a happy one. God led me to a passage from Isaiah. It read:

> He ploughed it and took out all the rocks and planted his vineyard with the choicest vines. He built a watchtower and cut a winepress in the rocks. Then he waited for the harvest, but the grapes that grew were wild and sour and not at all the sweet ones he expected.' (*Isaiah 5:2, TLB*)

I suppose that was it, really, in a nutshell, and it illustrated the heart of my exhaustion and growing dissatisfaction. I considered how Mary, myself and our team had worked so hard at 'ploughing' the ground God had given us. It certainly should be fertile, and there was no denying the need for evangelism with only about 3 per cent of the parish population involved in any sort of church. At St B's we had planted 'the choicest vines': in other words the teaching and worship was biblical and renewed. And yes, we did look for a fine crop of 'sweet grapes': soundly convened enthusiastic ongoing Christians. Yet all we seemed to have (at that point) were 'wild grapes': new Christians, yes, but reflecting their often difficult backgrounds; new converts still lacking self confidence and self-esteem – problems so indicative of the area. The results were unreliability, irresponsibility, lack of commitment and living on the level of feelings. Many folk were so full of their own needs that they found it difficult to see beyond themselves.

Yes, I could see the parallel, and then I realised that environmental norms could not be changed overnight. It would be a long process for the 'wild grapes' to become the exciting, dynamic, confident Christians I longed for, if ever! From God's answer, I saw that I was not to be the 'owner' of a successful mega-church, but the nurturer of 'wild grapes', slowly and patiently leading them onwards. Surely such a position is true for many leaders, yet the lack of results is so hard to cope with. And moving on to where the grass appears greener, rather than staying at the forefront of the battle, becomes very desirable.

I drove back home through rush-hour Birmingham; frustrated when I started out from the convent, and even more frustrated when I hit traffic. Why do car drivers go so slowly in heavy traffic? Why do they seem incapable of merging with cars from the right in one-way systems? Why does my lane always move more slowly than the other? Can I beat that BMW away from the lights? Why should cars be allowed to turn right against the traffic – especially when I'm behind them? Then I thought, 'This is a living parable of my life. I want everything to happen yesterday; to be clear for the big "me".'

McDonalds came up on the left, so I tugged my dog collar out, and swung in. Sometimes life is just too hard, isn't it?

I spent the next week swinging between hopefulness because the church was growing, and gloom because of the 'wild grapes' perception. If only I could take notice of my own sermon: 'Don't live on the level of feelings, but upon the truth of God's word.' I muttered one or two dark innuendoes about 'flaming grapes' to Mary, who merely raised her eyebrows in an unhelpful way. It seemed to me that whatever we did, however hard we worked, we'd still be banging our heads against a brick wall. If God had said that's how it was, then that's how it was. There was nothing we could do about it except keep on working, getting more and more exhausted.

16

Timid Tabbies, Cute Kittens and Toffee-nosed Toms

Tell the people... what their sins are.

Micah 3:8, GNB

'Oh no, Lord! I can't tell her that!' I prayed silently. 'What if I've got it all wrong? I'll look a real fool.' In my Quiet Time the Lord Jesus seemed to give me an inner understanding of the situation I was about to face. Was this really a word of knowledge, or was it my vain imagining? Self-doubt is a continual enemy of the Christian minister. On the other hand, so is unthinking arrogance. Yet I felt a wonderful sense of excitement flowing into my inner being – something expressed by the psalmist when he says, 'Deep calls to deep.' (*Psalm 42:7*) God was speaking into the depth of my being from the depth of his love. I decided that it was a word of knowledge and must be delivered.

The previous day I'd received a surprise telephone call from a woman named Maggie. 'Vicar,' she said confidently, 'I'm a Christian, you know. I used to go to a cinema in London. So I know all about Jesus. Can you help my friend Jane?'

'A cinema? What do you mean?' I responded.

'Our fellowship – it met there. On Sunday mornings. In the cinema.' As she explained, her mind was clearly on other things 'But it's Jane, you see. She's a hostess. In the nightclub with me. In Birmingham.'

She talked in staccato phrases, and I began to get the picture. But what did I know about nightclubs and hostesses, except that the latter were generally very pretty and sophisticated-looking girls?

125

'I heard how you helped Kim,' she continued, 'so can you come with me? To see her? You see, she's really messed up. Can I come and get you? Tomorrow?'

Maggie arrived on time and off we went in her sports car. The front garden of Jane's council house (council house for a hostess?) was in a dreadful state. Old mattresses had been thrown down and everything was totally unkempt. What a mess! As I walked tentatively down the path, I noticed the glazed front door was smashed, jagged edges smeared crimson. Beneath lay a congealed pool of blood strewn with glass fragments. There seemed to be hundreds of children around, playing and screaming in the midst of the chaos. Maggie walked comfortably before me and pushed open the shattered door.

'Jane? Jane? Are you there?' she shouted above the noise of the children. I half-hoped she wouldn't be.

Inside, the house was worse than the garden. And then there were the cats. They were everywhere: in the hall, on the stairs and even cluttering the sofa. There were timid tabbies, cute kittens and toffee-nosed Toms all over the place, as was obvious from the feline odours.

Jane greeted us with effort, looking at me through lifeless eyes. She was clearly in the middle of a personal crisis and in no mood to be nice to vicars. Though unkempt she was very attractive. 'Sit down, why don't you?' she said in a fairly offhand way.

I sank into the dirty sofa, scattering the cats. What should I do now? Talk about the weather? How could I cope with this contrast of personal beauty and sordid environment? And what about the broken door? There must be a story behind that. I took my heart in my hands and spoke out: 'Jane, I don't really know anything about you. But I want to tell you what I think the Lord said to me in my prayers this morning. It was all about you.' Despite the hard and callous expression that appeared on her pretty face, I explained the sense of what God had shown me about how she was feeling deep inside: her inner distress; her deep personal loneliness; her sense of separation and bitterness.

'It's not what I'm thinking myself,' I assured her, 'but what I believe the Lord wants to say to you.' I had no way of knowing whether any of my remarks were touching her at all, or if, in fact, she was thinking me a fool or fanatic. I felt like both, even as I was speaking.

Nevertheless, I continued: 'Jane, it's no good you trying to kid yourself everything's OK, because you know it isn't. Your life's breaking down, and just look at your kids. It's not right, is it? Anyway, where's God in all this? And I know you do believe in him, don't you?'

June blinked. 'How did you know about me?' she said in a tiny voice, as if totally shaken. The hard expression still masked her feelings, but there was a sense of God breaking through. After a short time, Maggie and I got up to leave, without even hearing her story. It was as if God's agenda had taken over.

'Jane,' I remarked as we reached the door, 'here's my telephone number. Ring me if you want to take this further.'

I longed to stay on and continue our talk, but somehow we all realised it was important for her to have space. My job for the moment was to trust God; to leave her to him and to pray. Any further initiative had to come from Jane, and from God's calling into her heart.

* * *

The current phase of growth was continuing, yet it was an odd sort of growth. It would be hard to call it evangelism in the conventional sense, because the people all came to us, but it was the most dynamic type of evangelism I've ever known because the people were God-given. They were all 'need centred' in the first instance, but they soon discovered that Jesus was the only answer, even though he offered the 'narrow path' rather than the degrading lifestyle many had known before. And the important issue was always being straight with them and helping them understand why the need had arisen and what they could do about it. Repentance and faith in Jesus Christ was the start of a lifelong journey of restoration.

Two weeks after our visit to Jane's house the telephone rang.

'This is Jane,' the subdued voice said. 'Do you remember me? You know – Maggie's friend.' Then she burst out, 'Luke's been knocked over. He's really bad. He's in intensive care. Can you come down?'

Luke, her six-year-old son, 'died' four times during that crucial period. Each time, the medical staff restored him to life. Then it was a further four long hours before the doctor appeared and told us, 'I think he has a chance now, although I must tell you we are concerned about possible brain damage. You must be prepared for that. It was a very serious accident.'

I called into the hospital the following day, and Jane whisked me into the ICU. Her little boy lay covered in sophisticated equipment, just emerging from the coma and beginning to respond in a hopeful way to his mother. How tender he looked as we prayed at his bedside just as we had prayed in the chapel during the terrible period of waiting the previous day.

Some days later Maggie, Jane and I sat down. Jane looked thoughtful as she started to speak. 'Wallace, all this about Luke, and what you said to me back at my house. It's made me think. I don't know how you knew those things, but they were all true. And Luke – when he woke from the coma, the first thing he said was, "It's God that made me better!" Why should he think that? He doesn't know anything about God. I really think it's a miracle; he's not even going to be brain damaged. Isn't that amazing?'

Jane went very quiet for a moment. Her words were obviously carefully considered as she declared, 'I've decided I don't want things to be like they were before. I don't want the kids growing up like me. You won't know this, but I used to be a massage girl. I worked at one of those parlours down by the shopping centre. It had a reputation for easy sex, and it was true because I used to be a star attraction.'

She went on, 'I quite enjoyed it all because I never got personally involved. I mean, it seemed all right, just giving men what they wanted. But sometimes when I really thought about things, I knew I felt dirtier and dirtier. So I pushed it all to the back of my mind. Later on, I began to get on well with the boss, so I started to run it all for him. It was good in some ways, you know: plenty of money and we lived in a lovely house. And then he asked me to run the blue cinema as well. It just seemed a natural thing to do.'

She paused then continued, 'Then I got married to the boss – Alec he was called. A really nice guy, except that he was into drugs and could change character in a moment, and then I felt he hated me. So I never knew where I was, but at least I had plenty of money.'

Jane's expression changed as the story progressed. The memories were becoming increasingly painful and her face clouded over. 'Well, it's a long story,' she sighed. 'Alec was in a very bad car smash, and then he died because of all the drinking. It was his liver. And all the money went to his first wife. So suddenly I was out on the street again, with nothing. I've always had a lot of bad luck.'

There was silence for a moment. 'After a bit I met this other guy, but he's a swine, and that was his blood you saw all over the front door. He'd tried to get in that night... well, it was about three in the morning. The children were terrified, but he was so drunk he didn't really know what he was doing. He didn't even notice us slipping out the back door. Then you and Maggie came next morning.'

It was as if God had opened the floodgates of her life. And the story poured out, far too much for me to take in at that point.

'I'm coming to your church on Sunday. Can we talk again please?' she asked as I stood up, exhausted, and ready to go home.

Mary later declared forcefully, 'There's a lot of work to be done now with Jane, don't you think?'

'Eh, what do you mean?' I replied. 'God's done it all, hasn't he?'

'Well, no, I don't think so. You haven't told her what her sins are yet. You told me earlier that she thought she'd just had a lot of bad luck. It was only circumstances that had spoiled things.' Mary used her teacher voice: 'If you leave her now, she'll be no better than when she started. She doesn't even begin to understand what her sins are. And anyway, she hasn't given her life to Jesus yet, has she? You haven't even told her that she needs to. Don't you see? There's a lot of work to do.'

'Don't you see?' is one of Mary's favourite expressions. When I hear it, I know I'm in for trouble. And she was right; there was an enormous amount of work to be done in Jane's life as events were to prove. And it wasn't only with Jane, but also Jim and quite a few others who were on the threshold of faith and needed so much help.

Reflecting back I can now see what was happening. The church was growing; growing in an almost unheard-of way for an outer-estate church. In the church-planting days of my early ministry, I had witnessed some relatively rapid church growth within the middle-class area of my 'patch'. However, those new converts were empowered people. They had a good educational and stable family background, and were well used to taking responsibility for themselves and others. It was easy to create support groups and for people to learn from each other and from the Bible about dynamic Christian living.

However, in this church most of the new converts had traumatic histories of physical, sexual or emotional abuse. Financial problems abounded; not the controlled debts of the empowered, but 'loan shark' confusion around an already marginal benefit income. Some had problems with reading at even the simplest level, so it was little help to study the word together; in fact it could be alienating. On top of their normal needs, spiritual problems needed dealing with, but we had to be careful in the use of our language. The very suggestion of evil spirits could do untold damage to folk whose self-esteem was already low, yet that issue certainly needed tackling, as I will recount later.

The command to 'tell the people... what their sins are' (*Micah 3:8, GNB*) was resulting in a church with a profound and growing ministry among the poor and needy. It was like a door opening in a person's life, through which ministry had to be poured so the past could be sorted out. We began to note the consequences on their children, which opened yet another aspect of the transforming work of the Holy Spirit. It was all or nothing. But then Jesus said, 'Anyone who does not take his cross and follow me is not worthy of me.' (*Matthew 10:38*

17

Children Are People Too

For God's promise was made to you and your children.

Acts 2:39, GNB

Children are people too. Even Freddy. Especially Freddy.

Freddy had a wonderful technique both to deal with children's church and to get attention. He would make his way to the furthest corner and simply stand on his head. For the whole period. Or if, for some totally unknown reason, he wasn't in head-standing mode, he would pinch and torment and possibly punch the nearest person while loudly proclaiming his absolute innocence.

His natural father was in prison for armed robbery, using a sawn-off shotgun, and he had a history of violent attacks. His older sister was, at that time, a prostitute on the streets of Birmingham. His mother had recently become a Christian, and time and time again we would claim, alongside her, that wonderful biblical pledge, 'For God's promise was made to you and your children.' (*Acts 2:39, GNB*) It is a sound biblical truth that Jesus died to save Freddy every bit as much as his mother or father or sister. Children are people too, and not just church appendages to be kept reasonably happy (or unhappy, as the case may be) in some dark, drafty, marginalised area while the adults get on with the 'real' worship.

In my 'placement' church of college days, a very old lady was left to cope with a dozen very modern children. She found that bribery with sweets and chocolate was the only method of control. She was a sweet, very Christian woman, totally out of her depth. But she reasoned that if she left her post, the whole of the children's work would collapse. Perhaps she was right. But it showed such a dire frailty of understanding by that congregation. And, yes, that church was dying!

So often our churches are orientated around the adult congregation, as if they are the ones who really count. In the Anglican church, children are not counted as part of the USA (Usual Sunday Attendance) figure. They are not part of the real membership (counted either through electoral roll or confirmation). They are not allowed to take communion, even though they have been baptised, until they come of age to be confirmed. Sunday school is often not in the 'real' church where the 'real' worship goes on. Surely children are just as able to truly worship as adults. Perhaps more so than many!

I once heard a respectable churchgoing lady put over very clearly, if inadvertently, many churches' attitude to children: 'I think it's good to see so many children in the Sunday school. After all, they are the church of tomorrow.' That same behatted lady could easily have turned round stiffly when those children made a noise during the together time in the service, looked at them coolly, then at the parent, and afterwards raised her eyebrows to her neighbour with a slight sniff!

I heard of a churchman in a small village congregation who, after noticing that a newcomer's two children were disruptive to the traditional fare, asked a neighbour what could be done. His friend replied, 'Oh, it's all sorted out. The churchwarden had a quiet word with them and told the mother that our church wasn't suitable for children.'

At St B's we have a policy to rejoice in the children. Our principle is that they are co-equal with the rest of the congregation. All of us are the church of today! Together we share part of the service and then separate into 'adult church', 'children's church' and 'youth church' in different parts of the church complex.

For us, the term 'Sunday school' was the first question. Surely our children come to church, just as we do, to worship the Lord. Of course, some children are far from a living relationship with Jesus, but then so are many adults. So we (or rather the children) chose the term 'children's church'. It is necessary to split up because we all need different types of teaching. But that is no reason to suggest that the 'important' church is the adult variety. Little wonder so many children leave the church when they approach teenage years after being pushed to one side as if they were second class.

'The church of tomorrow' is such a horrible saying. Of course children are the church of tomorrow, but they are also supremely part of the church of today! Within our church family, each section of the church is taught to respect the others, their different needs and pleasures. 'Adult church' has to learn that today's children are quite noisy and behave differently even from those of a decade ago. 'Youth church' and 'children's church' have to learn that most adults need quieter times, and also a different sort of music. I have little time for churches that are 'targeted' specifically at the youth culture or 'yuppies' or even the over-60s. Christ calls us to be a family, with all the consequential noise, mess and potential problems. I'm delighted with a church that has people who can't read, people with first-class degrees, folk on benefits, lawyers, people of all colours, children, those who are disabled, people with obvious needs, youths with Mohican haircuts, working men, women who are making headway in their career and mums looking after their children all by themselves. That is the wonder of the church of God. We are not a club for the similarly minded, but a fellowship of seekers and Christ's disciples longing to see the establishment of God's kingdom on earth.

The principle of seeing our church children as people in their own right has profound implications. When we arrived, the children's work was mainly aimed at keeping the attendees happy for an hour or so, with games and repetitive Bible stories, without considering the spiritual implications. How easy it is to immunise children against church by subjecting them to a product with minimal spiritual value. Yet little could be done because there were few spiritually alive members who could offer their gifts and services to the children.

As new young families met with Christ and committed themselves to the church, they began to ask questions about the Sunday school. One of the young mothers said, 'If my Saul has to hear the story of the Good Samaritan once again, I think he'll explode. He must have heard it a hundred times, and he's only nine.' She looked slightly repentant. 'Of course you have to teach Bible stories. But what our children need most is "faith learning". We've got to show them that Jesus is alive and active *now*, so they learn to live with him. But all we do is send them off to the coldest and scruffiest parts of the building, telling them yet another Bible story and then setting them to work colouring everything in sight. Where's the faith in that?'

It was desperately hard to harness the parental talents of the new Christians to teach the children what they themselves were learning about the Saviour! And anyway, we soon realised that it was foolish to send these new Christians into the then Sunday school each week, because they needed adult teaching and worship themselves. There was no easy answer.

However, as the church grew, the establishment of a simple rota system became very easy. And far more people were ready to volunteer when they realised that commitment to Sunday school was not every week for the rest of their lives! In fact, we offered them one month on, then two months off. And it didn't hurt the children to have different leaders each month; rather it extended the size of 'family' relationships. One mum subsequently took charge of the whole affair, changing the name to children's church, and even started to produce simple worksheets since all the commercially available teaching material appeared to be aimed at middle-class children with good biblical knowledge and advanced reading and writing skills.

Growing spirituality was the key factor. People began to realise that the children had spiritual potential, just like the teenagers and adults. They could meet with Jesus Christ in their hearts in a sane and relevant way. All three of my children are committed Christians, and each one of them has decided to commit and then re-commit their life to Christ through various stages of growth. One of them was given the gift of tongues at the age of ten, and all of them showed a wonderful Christian maturity through their adolescent years. Children are spiritual beings! They can receive Christ as their personal Saviour and experience the ongoing power of the Holy Spirit in their lives.

'It was amazing,' remarked the astonished young man who had just finished leading one of the children's groups. 'They were praying for me! They actually had 'pictures' and prophecies and one of them prayed in tongues!'

One ten-year-old lad shared with me: 'The group is great. We really meet with the Lord. I love it. We're starting our own home group tomorrow night, and Mary's going to tell us all about how God grew this church.'

Some people are still surprised to see a church leader disappear with the children into a warm hall. 'It's showing what we believe by what we actually do,' I commented. 'The kids need to see "upfront" leaders out with them.' Even the whole music band goes with them from time to time. Nobody can say that the children are second class. We now have a full-time children's worker, fully funded by various Christian charities. Faith can provide finance when God is breathing his Spirit over the work.

The often painful time of adolescence is exactly when we need our Lord. But if churches remain stolidly indifferent and marginalise the children's and youth work, then they fail them totally. Adolescence is often highlighted for the first time when children move from junior school to secondary school. For some, their home group may prove to be their anchor.

Four children in our church had chosen different secondary schools and felt very apprehensive as September approached. 'Let's make a pact,' suggested Ross. 'Each of us prays for the other three. Then when we meet up we can see what's happened.'

'That's cool,' retorted Philip Knox. 'How about we pray over the telephone if one of us has trouble?'

So the four secondary school boys faced the future knowing that Jesus was Lord of their individual situations, and that they had physical and prayer backup ready for the undoubted difficulties.

Spirituality in everyday life is not merely for full-time church leaders, or even Christians seeking to bring God into their workplace or home. It is also a key issue for growing children. Out of a population of over a quarter of a million, fewer than 300 children aged 16 and under attend an Anglican church in the Birmingham outer estates. And that number includes a large contingent from St B's! Now take away from that figure the youth and children who are mere casual attenders, and you see the puniness and slenderness of the spiritual resources we are offering to a quarter of the population of Birmingham. The same is probably true of most other major cities. Often other denominations have no presence on the estates. and even if they do, their track record is rarely any better.

As time has gone by, quite a few children from the church have formed their own home groups for Bible study, prayer and fellowship. The children have ministered to adults and other children and they've even gone out on mission. They are a totally underused resource of the church.

* * *

Out in the community the question of how to deal with children from difficult backgrounds on the outer estates was still paramount. The church, even with its vision and growing band of helpers, was merely touching a very low percentage of the need. Our local children and young people needed so much more.

I brushed the snow off my coat and reached for the security intercom button. Simultaneously the door burst open as a child, completely intent on some mysterious mission, rushed past me. Catching the swinging door, I ruefully reflected how easy it was to enter the safety-conscious school. I remembered how the Head had shared her continual, and quite justified, worry about personal attack. Indeed, some months previously she'd been assaulted by the angry boyfriend of a single-parent mother.

The school assembly went well. It generally did. And the children were smiley and nice. But on looking round I noticed once again how many of the kids seemed small for their age, and were dressed inadequately. Dirty tee-shirts and under- or oversized summer dresses matched the worn-out cheap trainers. I involuntarily shivered at the thought of 'home time' through the January slush.

The Head was waiting to express her latest anxiety: 'It's the new fashion of sex games that worries me now. Right here in my playground. And some kids seem to know everything: all the deviations, all the words, all the touching spots. And they "play" with each other. You wouldn't believe what they do sometimes.' Her passion and concern burst out. 'They know everything,' she repeated, 'and yet almost nothing about proper relationships and caring and "huggy" love. It feels hopeless. I see some of the mothers, Wallace, and you wouldn't believe how they swear at their children. And discipline is often just shouting or hitting. How can we teach them in such an environment? It's a continual uphill battle, and soul destroying for the caring parents.'

'Yes,' I agreed. 'Look at the Robertsons. They hardly got any sleep last weekend because neighbours had loudspeakers hanging out of the windows for their street party. When the mother tried to move young Cindy into the back bedroom, her asthma immediately flared up because of the damp. And baby Cherry's been in hospital three times already. All they can say is, "Keep her away from the damp." But how can they? Those houses are riddled with it. It's ridiculous.'

As I got more involved with those poor scraps, I realised it wasn't just a physical problem. Again there was that stunting of the mind and the spirit, leading to a soulless community. As people had turned their backs on God, so the place had become a breeding ground of poverty, broken relationships and jail. The darkness outside the church was still prevalent.

One day I unexpectedly received a letter from the Assistant Bishop of Birmingham: 'My dear Wallace,' it read, 'I write to confirm that you are duly allocated a deacon… Hilary has been a nursing sister for several years and is very experienced… I feel she would relate particularly well to the people on your… outer estate.' It appeared that the diocesan bishop, on his visit to St B's, had been deeply moved by the obvious plight of children at the school and the needs of so many single-parent mothers on the state. He rightly discerned that the authority of ordained female ministry was needed.

Some months later, my new colleague arrived with a special responsibility to work in that difficult area of the parish. Even today it remains hard and unfruitful. We are still praying, while becoming more and more involved in the frail social fabric of the community. We are learning to be part of that broken area so the light of Christ can be revealed. It's sheer hard, and often unrewarding, work. God's church has to grasp the nettle.

At one time we tried our hand at an 'open' youth policy for the community. It quickly proved to be unhelpful and even destructive...

'Don't mention youth to me,' I smouldered angrily as I joined Mary in the kitchen. 'My computer's gone, as well as my printer and all the software. Then there's the shattered windows, broken doors, stolen guitar and other instruments. And that horrible 666 stuff daubed on the eaves. Everybody is talking as if the kids out there are little angels. "All they need is something to do and somewhere to go,"' I parodied in a sarcastic tone. 'Don't talk to me about youth. That's the last time we try to start up an open youth club round here, I can tell you. All they were doing was "casing the joint".'

'OK, OK.' Mary raised her hands and shrank back mockingly.

I pretended to sip my coffee.

'You're sulking about the robbery,' she remarked with a smile. 'But you've forgotten about the work within the church family youth. It's easy to be negative, isn't it?'

I skulked around the kitchen, slamming a few doors and dramatically brooding for effect. It had been very important to allow some church members to do their own thing in starting up an open youth club, even though I felt very wary. Of course, the consequences of their inexperience in dealing with the young people of such a difficult area fell on me. Sometimes leaders just have to allow mistakes to be made, otherwise we become despots. Besides; all of us learn by experience. I calmed down, with a returning awareness that the church youth group was growing significantly.

God was clearly pointing us towards building up the spirituality of our church youngsters. The needs of the streets would come later, we thought, as we gradually developed a right spiritual base for the youth within the church at St B's. In fact God was leading us in a very different direction. We were about to discover that his heart was towards the children and young people who gathered in gangs down on the Valley. Their behaviour had a darkening effect on the whole of the community. And God was about to show his hand...

18

Trouble Valley

I will... make Trouble Valley a door of hope.

Hosea 2:15, GNB

'I've heard this area is rich in birdlife,' enthused the man in green wellies as he fingered his expensive-looking binoculars. 'Can you advise me on the particular species common to this habitat?'

Mary and I were bravely taking our dogs for a walk in the Woodgate Valley Country Park. As mentioned, it's rightly advertised as a beautiful area with a pleasant little stream called Bournbrook bubbling its way through the centre. Unfortunately, it is also sandwiched between two large outer estates known as Woodgate Valley North and Woodgate Valley South. Almost inevitably, rivalry grew up between the youngsters of the two localities, with conflict centred over the 'ownership' of a certain bridge across the stream.

We looked at the ornithologist for a moment, trying to decide whether he was sincere. I silently enquired of Mary, 'Is this guy for real?' Her eyes confirmed that she thought he was genuine. Clearly he had believed the prominent advertising extolling the rural virtues of the area.

I shrugged my shoulders because I really don't know much about birds, except that we have a profusion of magpies in our back garden. 'Over there is the quietest area,' I suggested, 'so it's probably the best place for birdlife.'

I went on to recommend he make sure of his exit well before dusk.

A few evenings previously, in the lounge of a house overlooking the Valley, I watched as smoke gushed up from a burning car. There was the sound of motorbike engines revving as they were ridden noisily along an impromptu track. I saw a father dash out and snatch up his child as the bikers enjoyed their illegal game. Another neighbour was dumping household rubbish just outside our friends' house (rather than his own back gate); it would be an eyesore and health hazard for weeks to come until the council spent yet more money on clearing it up. Should we report the fire? Should we report the bikers? Should we tackle the illegal dumper and receive the inevitable abuse? We opted for a 999 call to the fire brigade, closed the curtains and settled down for a cup of coffee.

Police sirens had always been a frequent summer sound from the 'area rich in birdlife'. 'There they go again,' the weary locals would comment, some hoping their children had not been involved in the fight for 'bridge ownership' this time.

This particular year, a group of delighted, excited teenagers emerged from the Valley and regrouped ready for the trip to the chippie. Along the way, lay a pleasant private cul-de-sac. Angry residents looked on anxiously as the gang raced through.

'This is just crazy. Surely something can be done?' somebody muttered as stones and even half a building brick were hurled at windows. With whoops of delight, others in the gang snatched up empty milk bottles and smashed them down violently. Some yelled abuse or scrawled graffiti. One of our church members had her back fence torn down and destroyed, causing her deep distress on top of the obvious inconvenience and cost. Of course, the people of the cul-de-sac were overwhelmed with outrage and continually called the police. Some even gathered to form a vigilante group, and others just wept. What a place to live.

The authorities continually sought to regain control of the Valley, sending in mounted police. The horses looked very grand as they meandered through the area, and no doubt they enjoyed the exercise with the added bonus of a cool drink from the stream. However, it was soon apparent that their presence added to the general 'fun' and even attracted gangs from another council estate two or three miles away.

The dog handlers moved in next. The police dog training school is nearby, so that seemed a sensible idea. 'They must be joking,' said one resident. 'The dogs will never be allowed to do anything with those kids around. The police would be absolutely crucified by the press if one got bitten. And the kids know it!' Another would make the point, 'Anyway, most of our lot are well used to roaming dogs, with even Rottweilers running free, so it's no threat anyway.' They were right. Soon the handlers and their charges were seen no more.

'Look at that helicopter!' Mary exclaimed. The noise was terrific as it hovered over the troubled area, searchlight probing into the gloom. It was quite frightening and one could feel the tension grow in the community. Was this answer any better than the mounted police or the dog patrols? We thought not.

Of course. St B's itself was equally impotent in the early days. At first it only dimly perceived its role as the spiritual heart of the estate. It took years of teaching and preaching the gospel before we were in a position to seize the initiative out there in the community. Yet how should the church respond? Time and time again I've sat in various church meetings with otherwise godly people moaning about the impossibility of their real-life situations, as if the whole answer rests on their shoulders rather than in the courts of the living God. There is such sheer strength in Psalm 127:1: 'Unless the Lord builds the house, its builders labour in vain.'

We discussed the problem in the Ministry Support Team, and perceived that our initiative into the Valley problem must arise out of the Red Sea Syndrome teaching and be owned by the whole fellowship. Here's what happened…

* * *

'Perhaps we should go and "put angels" on that bridge,' suggested some bright spark at Praise and Prayer as we sought a solution.

'That's a good idea,' responded a friend. 'If it worked round the church walls, why shouldn't it work down there?'

Our now swelling fellowship group was obviously increasingly angry about the way the prevalent youth culture was dominating the Valley.

'We've got to do something,' added another. 'It's as if Satan's main grip on the area is focused down there. It's wrong and ungodly.'

Mary spoke up. 'But God told us to "put angels on the walls". He hasn't told us to do any such thing down there. It sounds like a good idea, but you know what we always say about good ideas…'

She continued: 'But your thought of praying on location seems spot on. After all, prayer in the actual situation is a fundamental Christian principle, so we can't go wrong. Anyway, something inside me really responds to it. I think, maybe, it is God's way forward to go and proclaim his name right on the bridge – in the middle of the troubled area. All of us, together. In public this time!'

Silence descended on the group.

'After you, Mary,' said one helpful comedian.

We all looked at each other.

'Yes, that's got to be right!' exclaimed Maureen.

'Sounds good to me,' said somebody else.

I felt quite elated and had that profound sense of God inspiring our conversation.

'We'll have to preach the word down there, you know. By the brook,' offered another enthusiastic voice from the corner.

I swallowed hard as I realised it would fall to me. 'Would I be heckled?' I wondered.

'And Mary's absolutely right. It'll have to be all of us,' said another. 'The whole church needs to march down there to pray and worship on location. Publicly!'

My heart started to sink again. Publicly? So everyone knows? Even the bishop? Was this faith or was it folly? It certainly seemed to have the sense of God's hand upon it…

Maureen stormed into the church office on the day before 'the march'. 'Have you seen the headlines?' she demanded indignantly. 'Have you seen what they've put?'

The local paper had got hold of the story and emblazoned across the top of one page were the words:

CHURCH ACTS AGAINST YOBS

I was upset at the paper's stupid and unhelpful remarks. And clearly the 'yobs' themselves would not be exactly delighted. In fact one of our church families was directly threatened that unless they boycotted the event they would 'get done over'. Another mum was really scared about the consequences; she feared for her two children, but stoutly decided to continue.

As the procession drew near the entrance to the Valley, so an intimidatingly large group of local youngsters were lying in wait to 'sort us out'. I can still remember the sight of them sitting along a retaining wall, about 30 strong and ominously threatening. Should we turn tail? It was a scary moment. Yet conflict never came.

Instead of the silent, black-suited, pious, hands-together, religious people they expected, the young people suddenly found themselves surrounded by nearly a hundred colourfully dressed people of all ages. Banners were flying and many children were waving balloons and streamers as they frolicked around. Other folk were handing out leaflets explaining the reason for the march. Lively Christian music pulsated from the small lorry at the head of the procession. Clearly people were enjoying themselves and the atmosphere was festive. It was a moment of wonderment for me. I suddenly realised how the church had grown, both spiritually and numerically. My heart swelled, and inside I felt a wonderful sense of thanksgiving to God. Yes, St B's really had some life now, and we were spearheading the community.

But I still had to deal with the young people sitting silently on the wall.

It took courage to walk over to the assembled group: 'Why don't you come down to the bridge with us? We're going to sing and pray. You'd be really welcome.'

It was immediately clear that the 'yobs' were stunned. They were reduced to silence by the unexpected and, hopefully, spiritual power. Later, as we stopped the lorry at the bridge and began sorting out the sound system, many of them sheepishly appeared, some even taking a printed programme. As the worship songs begun, led by live music from a keyboard and electric guitar, so they sat on the bridge rails and joined in. What a moment! God was in our midst, and I'm sure he was smiling.

Mary said afterwards: 'The power of God was down there this afternoon. It was as if he were waiting for us to take the initiative and go right into the centre of the trouble.'

As I stretched out in front of the fire and stroked our Labrador, I totally agreed. Why, even my preaching had gone well and nobody had jeered or anything. 'It was good,' I stated. It was one of those lovely moments in ministry which seem to come only from a decision to do something 'daft' for the Lord.

* * *

Major gang disturbances in the Valley are a thing of the past. A statement by the police in the local newspaper the following summer said: 'This is the first summer when we have not been troubled with the teenage gangs… There was a time when 30 or 40 teenagers would attack each other with sticks and frighten local residents.'

The church march heralded a new era for our 'Trouble Valley', echoing Hosea's hope: 'I will… make Trouble Valley a door of hope.' (*Hosea 2:15, GNB*) We still have the occasional motorcyclist or wild, shrieking group, but these incidences are isolated. Cynics may say this is merely a coincidence, as they might in respect of the vicarage family trauma and 'angels on the walls'. However, we were experiencing again how dramatically the spiritual affects the physical. 'Coincidences' happen when God is invited into the situation. We have learned to call them 'God-incidences'!

Estate violence has clearly escalated these past years, yet few people see the connection with a growing godlessness within our society. However, a local school Head once said to me, 'Do you know, I'm beginning to think the biggest problem round here is not a lack of facilities. It's simply "undeveloped souls" within the children of our community.'

He was right. Our children need care and love and a stable environment. But above all, they need a rebuilding of the soul. They are not 'the enemy'. They are not 'the yobs'. They desperately need a spiritual dimension to life. Even the church, perhaps especially the church, is prejudiced against our young people. How we need to repent of such attitudes and look upwards into the face of our loving God for answers, rather than moaning and muttering about our problems.

Churches and schools have a terrific opportunity to work in partnership, each respecting the emphasis of the other. As we've prayed over our patch, God has opened up opportunities for teaching, assembly work and even three 'after school' Christian clubs. These clubs have the brilliant effect of teaching children out in the community about the Christian gospel. Of course, some years ago these state schools would have resisted any attempt by the church to get involved. However, a prayerful attitude, coupled with straightforward building up of relationships, has ensured a wonderful co-operative spirit. Most teachers are not 'anti-church', but some have had bad experiences of heavy proselytisation or just simply inept teaching skills, which have alienated church and school. Any opposition to the local church that does exist can be part of the dark blanket of Satan over an area, and must be prayed out.

It is of great interest that during a recent OFSTED inspection, one local state school was commended for its link with the church: 'Considerable emphasis is placed on the spiritual, moral, social and cultural development... this is a strength of the school.' It is so helpful that even our secular authorities are starting to gain understanding of the dire need for spiritual development within a community. In some places, it seems to me, the church needs to catch up with the world in its thinking.

19

The Helped Becoming the Helpers

Carry each other's burdens, and in this way you will fulfil the law of Christ.

Galatians 6:2

God uncovers his purposes in the most unexpected ways. Some years previously, as a curate, I'd taken the funeral of an elderly churchgoer. The circumstances had fashioned the backdrop to the tapestry God was already forming at St B's...

Two old ladies worshipped together at Anglican evensong.

'Good evening, Mrs Jones. Cold for this time of year, isn't it?' Mrs Smith rubbed her hands together as she sat beside her friend.

Mrs Jones answered as she moved slightly along the pew, 'Yes, it is chilly, isn't it?'

The conversation stopped. After all, church was church. And they both opened their prayer books... 'Dearly beloved brethren...'

The service ended.

'Well, good night then, Mrs Smith. See you next week as usual.'

It went on for 40 years, until one Sunday Mrs Jones didn't turn up. Mrs Smith waited patiently, little knowing that her 'friend' had died, quite alone, during the previous week. I discovered that their relationship of 2,000 Sundays had never progressed beyond the same old remarks. Maybe they knew God himself, but they certainly didn't know each other. And surely that was an insult to true Christian fellowship.

I determined that any church I led would be broken down into smaller groups to ensure such a situation never happened. However, the social structures (such as they were) of our outer-estate parish mitigated against any fellowship groupings.

For instance, Archie, a 70-year-old church member, just didn't know how to 'be friends'. He was alienated from all his children and grandchildren, and occasional family meetings consisted merely of cutting comments thrown at one another.

Another new Christian, Bev, had strong verbal fights with her neighbours every time they saw each other. 'Do you know, Wallace,' she told me with an incredulous grimace, 'all they do is jeer at me. "You b*** do-gooding hypocrite, always sucking up to the f*** vicar," they say. Just because I'm trying to get my life sorted out. And my mother, all she says is, "Well, you ought to keep yourself to yourself, just like I do." Why can't people understand?'

Jim and Marge had been so tied up in their domestic arguments that when they became Christians, they discovered they had no real friends. Jim shared their problem with me. 'Sometimes Marge and I don't know what to do with ourselves now we've become Christians. I mean, it's great when there's meetings and things. But other nights…?'

He looked quizzically at me. 'I think I've worked it out, Wallace. We used to watch all those videos – all the sex and violence we could get our hands on. And then we'd argue and shout at each other, or at the kids. Do you see? Our time was full. But now we want different things out of life, because of Jesus. We want Christian friends and all that.'

God was clearly showing us we had to create in St B's an alternative society; a new Christian grouping that would be easily joinable, and yet mould people together. So St B's 'Responsibility Groups' were born. These are home groups with a more vibrant character, where small clusters of people learn to be responsible to the Lord, his church and each other. They are places in which to focus ongoing pastoral care so there can be a sharing of lives among fellowship members; places where the helped can become the helpers.

On the outer estates, there is very little sense of community, but many elderly people reminisce about the sense of togetherness engendered within the older, often condemned housing from which they were rehoused. They will tell of the 'back to back' so-called slums where 'we were always popping in and out of each other's houses, and didn't even have to lock our doors. This nostalgic backview affectionately includes the communal outside toilet! One has the clear understanding, despite the sentiment, of a people facing the present and future together. Few could say such a feeling exists on today's estates, although there are pockets of love, trust and affection.

It is equally clear, at this raw edge of our postmodern generation, that the family structure, so beloved in those past days, has lost its power. The conventional lifestyle of married couple and children is extremely weak on the estates. As a result, traditional moral and spiritual values are ever becoming more and more flimsy. Yet, paradoxically, wider family relationships can have an almost destructive strength.

So Responsibility Groups on the estates need a different ethos from the home groups culture of the developing church scene. They have to fit the needs of a broken community and 'disempowered' Christians.

* * *

Nick told me a story from his Responsibility Group which well illustrates the needs and problems...

'Chaos tonight at our meeting. You remember Owen's daughter, the one with the "boyfriend"? Well, the phone rang just as we were starting, and she was shouting, "He's killing me! He's killing me!" Leanne and Tyrone were having a real bust up... again.'

He raised his eyebrows slightly.

'Owen said you could hear the furniture being thrown around in the background and he was really worried because Tyrone is a maniac sometimes. Why she doesn't finish with him I'll never understand. Anyway, four of us piled into the car to rescue her. And the rest stayed behind to pray. Owen directed me, but he got a bit mixed up and we went down the wrong street. Just as I was about to turn round, there was Leanne being chased by Tyrone, and she looked a right mess. So it was Responsibility Group to the rescue! Luckily Tyrone thought we looked too many to tackle, so he just skulked away.'

Nick looked thoughtful for a moment. 'One other thing. If we hadn't turned down the wrong road we would have missed them altogether, and who knows what would have happened? It was the rest praying, I think. And God knew the mistake would happen so he sorted it all out.'

Jim shared a story about his group: 'Carrie's never really invited anybody into her house, you know. It's not that she's been ashamed of it or anything like that. It's just the idea of offering hospitality to anyone other than close family has been totally beyond her idea of friendship. Yet time after time now, Carrie's opening up her home, thinking responsibly about the needs of others. She even had Jane and the kids for Sunday dinner the other week.'

Almost irrelevant in middle-class circles, but what a triumph for her and the Responsibility Group!

Marge also had a story to tell. She knew what it was like to be battered. In the old days, Jim had often taken his temper out on her. But now it was a member of her group covered in bruises and cringing away. Instead of running as she would have done in the old days, Marge put her arms round the girl and comforted her. She understood, and she knew exactly what to do, even when Fran sobbed, 'I just want him dead.' This was no 'official' counselling from a hundred times removed social worker, but responsible friendship in dire circumstances. She had said to Fran, 'Imagine your Rick is standing on the edge of a sheer cliff and the drop looks straight down to the needle-sharp rocks beneath. He is balanced right on the edge. He doesn't realise the danger and you can reach out and give him a little push – just a very little push and that'll be the end of it all, won't it? He won't be able to hurt you again. Are you going to do it, Fran? Are you going to push him?'

After a long pause Fran spoke. 'No,' she said. 'No, I'm not.'

So Marge went on, 'There you are then, you don't really hate him – you don't really want him dead. Now let's talk and pray about it.'

Marge had taken responsibility for another group member and had helped her deal with the resentment and hatred. She knew the needs from the inside.

The wonderful stories of groups being concerned for each other warmed my heart. Quite honestly I felt the glow of pride of a father when his children come of age and show their maturity with some selfless acts. The church seemed to spring to life on every side, and I think for that short time I felt genuinely happy and even satisfied (a dangerous emotion for a church leader, because you can so easily take your eyes off God). Members were even starting to look outward from their own established group to the wider needs of the church, and welcoming some newcomers.

A young professional couple were moving into the area to be part of a Christian outreach team into local schools. They'd hired a large removal van and spent all day loading up and then driving to Birmingham. Exhaustion was etched on their faces as they arrived.

Mary said, 'I'll always remember the astonishment on Eleanor's face as she saw our men waiting for them. There was Terry, complete with string vest and tattoos; Doug with beer belly hanging over his falling-down trousers and just that glimpse of bum; and a huge church member who worked as a nightclub bouncer. James and Eleanor just stood and gaped as their bannister rail and fitments were speedily disassembled, allowing wardrobes and beds to be whipped upstairs. Then the washing machine was lifted bodily through the hall with a "watch your back, m'duck". The van, which had taken literally hours to fill, was emptied in minutes. Even the bannister was reassembled in double quick time. Then, at the end, everybody gathered in the living room to pray. And here were these burly men pleading with Jesus to bless the house. Then the door closed and they were gone, leaving a totally astonished couple.' Mary went on. 'I should think it all seemed like a dream afterwards. It was lovely.'

The examples flowed and flowed. All over the fellowship, people were demonstrating responsible care. Not with complicated systems and intricate schemes, but with loving self-offering. I was thrilled to read the scripture: 'Carry each other's burdens, and in this way you will fulfil the law of Christ.' (*Galatians 6:2*)

Of course, my feeling of ease couldn't last. Our fledgling leaders were still veritable babes in many ways, and the vast majority of the congregation lacked the self-confidence and ability to take anything other than the first tentative steps. But for a moment it felt that we had somehow arrived.

Every church member was allocated to one of the Responsibility Groups whether they chose to be part of it or not. So quietly the whole pastoral dynamic of the church evolved into these small groups, where people were learning to be church and be responsible for each other. Some were even starting to take pastoral initiatives, like Terry and Doug helping our newcomers. In the background, the Ministry Support Team were quietly helping indigenous folk to take responsibility for each other. But instead of relieving the burden on the 'scaffolding', the need to develop leadership skills was increasing the overall workload. Certainly a new day was dawning, but it was so very difficult to see any sustained holding of responsibility. It seemed that years of disempowerment had led to a dependency culture where rights were paramount, but responsibility was still a pipe dream for many of our 'lambs'. Clearly the Lord Jesus Christ was breaking the unhelpful emotional and spiritual hold of their cultural backgrounds, yet I had little idea how to take people from this dependency to full independence, and until we could do so, the scaffolding would have to remain.

However, even as the pastoral dynamic was changing, the growing church was spawning more and more converts. The early Praise and Prayer meeting, which had been the background strength to the growth of the church, had to move out of the vicarage because of size. Almost immediately it lost its pioneer sense of purpose. and became a mere prayer and teaching meeting which was fast eclipsed by the growing power of our Sunday worship. It lost its identity. Again it was apparent that we were moving from 'small' church to 'middle-sized' in terms of church growth. We were losing that tight-knit sense of purpose.

The moment of grace seemed to be coming to an end, and big questions were on the horizon.

20

Painting a 'Faith Picture'

He was looking forward to the city with foundations, whose architect and builder is God.

Hebrews 11:10

With shoulders drooping, the outer-estate vicar showed me round his gigantic Victorian pile of crumbling red brick. The rain sleeted down, and the building looked as if it had always been there: always dirty, depressing and dismal. As we walked to the front entrance, water dripped from the overgrown bushes lining the pathway.

'We've got nobody to sort this lot out,' he murmured ruefully, brushing aside yet another sodden overhanging branch. 'And we've got to keep this fence,' he confirmed, touching the six-foot-high metal barricade across the old porch entrance. 'If not, the kids just use the area for dossing down, doing drugs and vandalising anything that stands. We have no choice.' It was a statement of the times, in his eyes.

Oliver was the archetypal 'one man band' vicar. He clearly loved the Lord and longed for something to happen, yet he was deeply depressed. The whole show, as he saw it, was on his shoulders. The members merely came and went on Sundays and occasionally made trouble at PCC meetings.

Inside, the 60-foot-high south wall bowed outwards, protesting its many years of non-maintenance. Buckets lined the floor around the pulpit, testifying, together with the resounding drip drip, to the state of the roof. The old flags hung limply, signalling a more prosperous past. I saw the despair in Oliver's eyes as he raised his hand in acknowledgement of the overwhelming problems. He paused for a moment as the personal pain of the dark, dank church seemed to consume his faith.

'My congregation's down to a handful now,' he lamented sadly. 'And most of them are very elderly. So I don't know what's going to happen. Perhaps the Lord's waiting for them to die so we can move forward. Perhaps mine is a "keeping" ministry.'

Oliver continued: 'We had the Christmas fayre the other week. It's the highlight of the year for all of our members. The tombola is so important they have a special cupboard for the prizes to be gathered over the year. And woe betide me if I dare to alter the position of any of the stalls. Or forget to thank certain people.' He flicked some dust from a rather musty-looking kneeler. 'It was good in the past, but now it's become a ritual.'

I saw anguish flicker across his face. 'I don't mind it so much. But it's what it all represents. That's what I find so disturbing. It's as if we're a stagnant backwater. And nobody will get involved, except in what's always been done.' He shuddered as he went on: 'This place is frozen in history. Things just survive. It's always been their way of life and way of church.'

Oliver had a subconscious model of the church, which deeply affected his ministry. Summed up, it was clergy and 'others'. The clergy ran the church for the benefit of the others. All sacrificial living was vicariously 'done' by the vicar! And it was he who ran the 'petrol station' where his church members could be refuelled each week. Of course, the PCC made decisions, but without the responsibility. After all, the church was his 'freehold'. On top of running the church, it was his responsibility to visit members, get involved with the local community, give communion to the sick, hold funerals and baptisms for the parish... and generally be nice to everyone.

The biblical model, however, is 'every member ministry': a situation where all people who claim to be Christians are called to be the church. Therefore 'being church' is a corporate exercise. Of course, all churches need leadership, but not so-called omnicompetent vicars. At St B's we had developed a good leadership team, but at the same time we were in danger of building a church totally reliant on that 'scaffolding'. Yet it was clear that God had developed our thoughts to start facilitating the helped to become the helpers, and that was working fairly well. However, we had the sense that God's picture of the church was much wider and more profound. It was obvious that our 'control' was limiting growth, yet how could we develop every member ministry, especially when so many of our folk were from a disempowered background?

Martin Thompson came up with the answer. We'd already found his prophetic gifting to be reliable, so when he came to the Ministry Support Team and offered his 'faith picture' we were completely ready. His face was shining as he started to share his thoughts. I felt excited even then. Mary wrote his exact words down: 'I saw a busy active large building site. I could see many people rushing about being extremely industrious in their own little sections. They were making many decisions for themselves, but working to an overall plan everyone was aware of. They were only concerned with their little bit, but all the activity was coming together as the emergence of a large building could be seen. Wallace had the plans of the building in his hands and was walking round the site checking the plans against the work. Occasionally he would stop and slightly correct something, perhaps a wall was out of true and he stopped to straighten it. The people were working in their own way, but in line with the plans of the building. Obviously they needed an overseer, but not a dictator.'

There was a growing conviction that this was of the Holy Spirit as Martin continued: 'And listen to the word I had alongside the picture: "I have taught you how to lay foundations. Now is the time to release others and teach them. You cannot do everything yourself. If you do not allow others to build, and do not care for them while they do so, they will move to another building site."'

'Martin, this fits in so well,' Mary pronounced with a grin from ear to ear. 'Do you see? The scaffolding is up all around the church, just like in Elizabeth's dream. But it's starting to rust into position rather than facilitate the building. It will soon become an end in itself.' She looked around the group. 'Do you see?' she said again with increasing gusto. 'Now is the time for the scaffolding to start to come down as the building goes up. Now is the time to open up a real building site using everybody in the fellowship.'

There was a murmur of growing excitement, except from me. 'You must be joking!' I exclaimed with a sinking heart. 'There's no way we can take all the scaffolding down. Everything we've been working towards would just collapse overnight. It would be chaos!'

My mind raced. 'Imagine,' I went on with growing wariness. 'Imagine who we would give jobs to.' I looked at Janet. 'Maybe Norma could become treasurer,' I said. 'She would enjoy sharing everything, don't you think? Just like she wanted you to share your cars!'

I continued with my gentle sarcasm: 'And Maureen, we could put Teri in charge of church cleaning. She'd soon whip the kitchen into shape. Just like her own!'

'How about Tom and Jean in charge of the Sunday creche?' I continued mercilessly. 'The toddlers would have a great time doing what they pleased!'

Unfortunately my complaint, far from helping my case, was causing the others to laugh uproariously. They certainly could imagine what would happen – only too well! Martin Knox added his own 'helpful' suggestion: 'I was thinking that Jane could become our chief welcomer. After all, she's had a lot of experience in the art of "welcoming" at her old nightclub. Or perhaps she could run our marriage preparation classes!'

By this time the meeting had descended into riot, with everyone stepping forward to give their own hilarious advice.

We had dipped our fingers into every member ministry with Responsibility Groups, and we had established the principle of the helped becoming the helpers – albeit weak and subject to failure. Normally that sense of weakness and failure tends to limit such an approach. But in the building site picture, God was clearly telling us to extend this principle, perhaps even against common sense, into the overall life of the church. The natural response was to back off because it can often lead to messy vulnerability: we knew people would mess up and perhaps create even more work for the already nearly burnt-out leadership team.

However, the very vulnerability of the building site concept helps us comprehend that no ministry or method or strategy need be complete or perfect in itself. Walls that are started can be knocked down again, things relocated to fit better. It is all slightly chaotic, but then so is life and so is any growing church! Leaders have a glimpse of the overall plan, but only God himself has the divine perspective. 'Now we see but a poor reflection as in a mirror,' said St Paul. (*1 Corinthians 13:12*)

Churches must learn to allow people to make mistakes. Otherwise we just hold on to what exists because it is safe. Often congregations lose the dynamic of faith through simple fear. Possibilities abound in any local fellowship, yet growth is often stunted because nobody will make leadership decisions in case they go wrong. Of course there must be constant checks in the background to ensure only the good and right is allowed to stand. But there is an organic rightness in human beings trying, making mistakes, trying again, and again and again. Has your church got hold of this principle, or is it sitting in stultifying safety?

Clearly our embryonic building site was already in existence, Responsibility Groups being part of it, but there were to be many other facets. New initiatives had to be constantly encouraged, even those we knew might well be half-baked. Many would fail, but then isn't that how all children learn? The children of God are no exception. We have to learn to walk, play and produce within the kingdom. So-called omnicompetent leaders lead their flock only to frustration and untimely death.

Martin Knox summed up the whole situation wonderfully, saying, 'You know, if Jesus had waited until all the disciples were ready, nothing would ever have happened. He even allowed Judas to be part of the learning team. That's real vulnerability.' He stated emphatically, 'We have to begin to release our people into ministry. There's no other way.'

I added thoughtfully, 'And if it works here, it can work anywhere.'

This was good. God's light in this dark area was to be channelled through God's building site, as members were given the opportunity to develop their ministry. That was surely the way to build God's kingdom base together. And not just in our particular location. Within me I had the sense of God's light spreading wider and wider, as his church authenticated the ministry of all believers. I was stirred and challenged for the future.

21

Does God Speak Through Dreams?

If the Son sets you free, you will be free indeed.

John 8:36

'Mary?' I caught her attention as I began to frame my question. 'Does God speak through dreams? What do you think?'

She raised her eyebrows as she continued to sort out her diary.

'Put that down for a moment,' I frowned at her. 'It's important. You know how Cynthia hasn't been responding to counselling? Well, I had a dream about her last night.'

The telephone rang. It always rings at crucial moments, just when I'm trying to get things sorted. 'Rev Brown, can you take a funeral next Friday at the crem?' asked the undertaker's secretary. I mechanically took the details, then returned to the breakfast table.

'In my dream, Cynthia had had an abortion.' I looked warily at my wife. 'Well? What do you think?'

'Why not? An abortion? It would certainly add up.'

Cynthia was desperate for a baby. The idea consumed her. How often she and her husband had been prayed for.

'Do you think this could be the problem? An abortion in her early years? Shall I go and confront her? 'The Lord told me about your abortion…' Can you imagine what would happen if I'm wrong? She'll completely break down. And even if I'm right, what'll happen then?'

I wasn't happy with my dilemma.

'Janice is the one who had the job of praying for her,' Mary commented. 'She seems to know everything about her now, so why don't we test the ground with her before you plunge in?'

After Janice had given me a vague nod to a vague question, Mary and I quietly met with Cynthia. As we chatted for a moment over coffee, I noticed once again her preoccupied air – as if her mind were too full to take any more information. I felt that any stray word could lead to a volcanic explosion, yet I was strangely compelled to ask the dramatic question. I just couldn't think of any genuine way to soften my words. So with heart beating wildly I simply said, 'Cynthia, did you have an abortion once? Perhaps when you were a teenager?'

What a reaction! First stunned silence and then, 'How on earth did you know that?'

'God revealed it to me in a dream,' I answered simply, as if it were the most normal thing in the world, whereas my true feelings were nearer to panic.

Cynthia broke down. The abortion had been her skeleton in the cupboard. She'd been refusing to admit the reality of her past, and wouldn't even allow her mind to consider the rights and wrongs of abortion. Yet her true feelings were complete distress and self-loathing, possibly as a result of Christian truth in her spirit.

Mary and I talked with her, for hours it seemed, going over the details again and again: the anger she felt; the self-loathing; the pain; the sense that she didn't deserve another baby. Then came the repentance, followed by a mini-funeral service for the deceased child. We laid its soul to rest, and at the same time gave absolution to Cynthia.

Sometime later, she had her much-wanted baby. Perhaps freedom from guilt was the key. Only God knows.

How chaotic lives can often be. We soon learn in ministry never to trust the obvious, and that even the more empowered people often have deep needs. As the psalmist says, 'The unfolding of your words gives light.' (*Psalm 119:130*) God's word was unfolded through this dream, bringing his wonderful light to Cynthia. But beware 'blueprints'. God works his wonders in *his* ways.

Maureen walked up smiling. 'There's three of them in the toilet, crying their eyes out.'

'Must be my sermon,' I thought proudly.

'It all started during the time of worship,' she went on. 'I noticed a couple of people getting upset. Then Jane. Then one by one they all went into the ladies. It's like a lake in there now.' Maureen looked pleased with herself. 'Jane wants a group of us to pray with her. She feels it's time – whatever that means.'

I responded, 'It's about a year now, isn't it? Since she became a Christian? I guess it's time for another step.' After all her terrible past and the near death of her son, Jane had finally met with Christ.

The following Thursday night a prayer ministry team of three met. As always, they began with a time of waiting on God.

'Jane?' Maureen looked at her carefully. 'I've had a picture that I think is especially for you. Let me tell you about it.'

Jane nodded her head.

'I saw you with a knife in your heart. And on the knife was written the word "unforgiveness". It was as if God said, "Tell Jane she's got to forgive. Nothing can be put right until she forgives and the resentment she feels is sorted out."'

Maureen continued, 'Now I've no idea what the problem is, but I'm sure it's having a major influence on your life. Does it make sense to you?' She sat back, as Jane leaned forward.

'It could be about my mother,' she said, stifling a lump in her throat. 'Do you think it could be?'

Mary said, 'Well, why don't you tell us about it? Then we can see.'

She started to cry as the harrowing story poured out. Later, under Maureen's leading, she forgave her mother, and the burden of personal bitterness for being abandoned as a young child lifted from her shoulders. The prayer ministry team sensed it was the beginning of a new, dramatic healing of the soul.

Jane is like so many new Christians from difficult backgrounds. She made a wonderful commitment to the Lord, but all the years of trauma had left their mark, and not only on her emotions. Hours and hours of using the sunbed in her massage parlour had taken their toll on her body. Years later skin cancer appeared and spread inwards. As I write, Jane has only a very short time to live.

I share the profound sadness of all the St B's fellowship in watching somebody we love die, riddled by such a terrible disease. The transforming Christ, through prayer ministry, has deeply changed Jane as a person: she wakes early and spends hours reading her Bible and speaking to Jesus. But the consequences of her former life still cling to her physical frame. Of course we have prayed and prayed and fasted and done all the right things, but the cancer is strong and growing. Perhaps she will never be whole until she reaches the eternal arms of her Saviour in heaven.

Jane does not stand alone. Because of the fractured society of today, many new Christians have to live with the consequences of past events in their lives. Those consequences could be illegitimate children by different fathers, problems with drinking or gambling, a deep lust for pornography, or even the knowledge that they have abused their children in some way. Judy, who had such a wonderful experience of Jesus at a Christian camp, still has ex-boyfriends hounding her and loan sharks on the front doorstep. Of course, these problems show their cutting edge in deprived areas, but they are symptomatic of a society that has turned its back on God. Again I stress how important it is for the local church to stand alongside these people by helping them through past traumas and preparing them for the future.

In Jane's case, her children are constantly cared for by friends at church during her prolonged periods of hospitalisation. Help is to be profoundly practical as well as spiritual. There is a wonderful, organic link between counselling, prayer ministry and straightforward practical assistance. Jane's children still bear the scars of past experiences, with problems like screaming nightmares, bed-wetting and general insecurity.

Yet often the church appears to stand aloof, wanting only to meet and praise the respectable, and exchange superficial banalities. Surely many parishes throughout the land have their Janes sitting in personal isolation, unable to express anything of the complex nature of their needs. Is it any wonder that many folk are turning to other religions for true spirituality when the church has side-lined reality for a sort of 'English' decency?

Prayer ministry is a helpful way forward. It's a dynamic way of bringing Jesus into real-life situations, especially into people's past. Yet even to begin prayer ministry requires a shift in thinking by many congregations. What we need is a life-changing vulnerability; a sense of God being at work; a joy in seeing people's whole personality being released by the power of the Lord. Prayer ministry can only flourish in a seedbed of faith!

At St B's we have developed teams to seek God's heart for others. However, the starting point is these 'helpers' coming out and being vulnerable themselves. They are not external social workers seeking to empathise, but caring friends who have welcomed the Lord within their personal troubles and who long to see him working in others. The recipient is never merely a client!

Above all, our helpers are people who know that the Spirit of God has power to transform. Of course they require training, experience and commissioning. That must be part of the lay leadership plan of the fellowship. They are key members of the congregation who are released to work on the building site. Very soon, some of the people they help become helpers themselves, and so the work grows. And as the people of the church see the practical results in people's lives, so they grow in faith.

Prayer ministry works! It is prayerfully seeking God's divine mind for someone. Often we use this ministry in parallel with counselling. In our church some of our pastoral assistants are trained counsellors and their skilled input is invaluable. Sometimes the prayer ministry stands alone and simply slices to the very heart of the need. Time and again we have discovered how God reveals the deepest needs within the hearts of his people: through dreams and pictures, and also through 'words' and straightforward Scripture passages, together with sanctified common sense. Often prayer ministry can culminate with the laying on of hands, anointing with oil or a celebration of Holy Communion. The purpose of such ministry is to break down the personal darkness that surrounds so many folk. Even committed Christians.

22

'It's My Mother. She Keeps Coming to See Me'

Your enemy the devil prowls around like a roaring lion looking for someone to devour.

1 Peter 5:8

Mary opened the front door to the insistent ring.

'Oh!' remarked the startled young lady standing on the step. She glanced at the man next to her. He nodded his head, so she said, 'I'm sorry, but we were looking for the vicar. Do you know...?' her anxious voice tailed off uncertainly.

The young man took over. 'It's my mother,' he said sheepishly. 'She keeps coming to see me. So Jilly and I wondered if the vicar could help?'

Mary tried not to look amused. She told me afterwards that she had visions of me 'warning off' Jilly's belligerent in-law. She merely replied, 'Oh, yes,' in an inviting way. 'Are you having trouble with her then?'

'Well, not trouble exactly,' the young man shifted his feet. 'You see, she's been dead two years.'

Mary told me over tea, 'I could hardly keep a straight face. I mean, he said it in such a matter-of-fact way. And the girl just stood there nodding her head. Anyway, I said you'd call round tonight. I hope that's OK.'

This strange doorstep request was to be the start of a sudden and unexplained catalogue of dark spiritual occurrences, right at a time when the church was growing strongly. Could there have been a connection?

As we knocked on their front door that same night, I saw the lace curtains move and a woman's disturbed face appear. She smiled nervously on seeing my dog collar.

'Come on in. I'm Jilly and this is my husband Steve. Thanks ever so much for coming round. We've been so worried, haven't we, Steve?' Steve looked embarrassed.

I introduced my team of three and then sat down.

'Do you think a front door can open on its own?' questioned Steve in a troubled voice. Maybe he wasn't expecting to be taken seriously.

'What do you mean, Steve?' I enquired.

Jilly took up the story. 'It's like the other night, Vicar. We were sitting here, on the settee, watching the telly, and we both heard the door open, didn't we, Steve?'

She paused for reassurance and he added, 'That's right. And when we looked, the front door was open, but there wasn't anybody there. It's happened a few times now. I've even tried to fix the latch to see if it can open itself. And Jilly will tell you, I'm really good at fixing things.'

They glanced at each other. Clearly their story wasn't over. I smiled sympathetically as Steve plucked up courage to start on the next bit.

'My mother, she was sitting there. On the chair you've got. And like I told your wife, she's been dead for over two years. I mean, Jilly and I saw her dead in the hospital and sorted the funeral and things. But she was there!' He pointed at the chair, earnest and confused, and then burst out, 'It keeps happening, again and again! What am I going to do? I just don't want her to come! I don't know what she wants! And she never says anything. What have I done wrong?'

Jilly slipped her arm round him as he became more and more emotionally distraught.

'What do you want us to do?' I questioned.

'Get rid of her!' he exclaimed desperately. 'I want you to get rid of the ghost. I want you to get things back to normal.'

Here was the rub. Over and over again I've found that people who have spiritual troubles are not the slightest bit interested in Jesus Christ or even God himself. It's rarely a faith matter – it's just a case of getting rid of the problem. I tried to explain how Jesus warns about 'sweeping out the house' and leaving it empty, but to no avail. They just wanted things to 'get back to normal'. So a situation like this is rarely an evangelistic opportunity, at least not in our short-term encounters. However, it does seem to be part of the power struggle over an area. Evil spirits hate the light emanating from God's people, and fight back in their halting, often ridiculous way.

Within the week we had another crisis on our hands. It began with a telephone call to the vicarage: 'Vicar, it's my daughter Kylie. She's in a terrible state. She just sits all day in the corner of our living room, hugging herself and sort of nodding her head backwards and forwards.' The distraught mother's words continued to pour out: 'She won't go to school either. I've had the doctor in, but he just gave her some Valium. It hasn't made any difference at all. Can you help? I don't know who else to turn to.'

I sent an experienced team to Annie and her daughter. The team leader reported: 'Apparently Kylie was sitting in the Valley waiting for her boyfriend. She felt a presence behind her and the sense of a hand touching her shoulder. On turning round she saw the horrible grotesque face of a repulsive old man. It was red and swollen all over, with blue patches and protruding, staring eyes. Biting into the swollen neck was a tightly looped length of thick rope. The apparition was dressed in old-fashioned clothes. Then, before her eyes, the 'ghost' faded away, leaving her coldly petrified.'

Kylie's story was made more credible by other reports of ghosts and ropes. One man told us of the panic he felt because he 'saw' what he described as 'hanging ropes' appear on the branches of a tree. A particular block of houses backing onto the Valley had three instances of ghosts and ropes. And in a nearby flat, a young girl died after being found hanged. I conducted the funeral.

We began to look into the past to see if there were any historical facts that could throw light on the situation, as part of a 'spiritual mapping' project. To our surprise, we were told that the Woodgate Valley used to be a stage coach route into Birmingham. The notorious heathland was a favourite haunt of highwaymen; a place of great and terrible fear. Further investigation revealed the site of a public hanging gallows, where highwaymen were executed. Could there be some sort of connection in the spiritual realms? Was it part of the reason for the darkness that hung over the area?

Later, we prayed with Kylie and set her free in the name of Jesus Christ. I rang her mother a week later to ask how she was.

'She's fine,' she answered peremptorily, without even bothering to thank us. I think she reasoned that it was our job, and therefore her entitlement. Like some sort of spiritual National Health Service. Neither Annie no Kylie came near the church during that time, or has been since. Yet it was a spiritual battle won: part of the ongoing conflict to defeat the enemy, even in his own stronghold.

After dealing with such problems, a profound tiredness often sweeps over me. It's almost as if my portion of spiritual energy has been overused. Also depression sometimes follows, perhaps because people don't appear to be any closer to the Lord, or it could be that a spiritual reaction is set up. Maybe a combination of both. Anyway, I find myself all too often immersed in a sense of profound failure.

* * *

'Vicar, I want them done,' demanded the ill-dressed woman as she called in the church office one Saturday morning. I assumed she meant infant baptism for the dirty bedraggled little girls beside her.

I questioned her: 'What's made you suddenly decide to come to church? After all, your children must be about three and four now?'

'They're not my children. They're our bab's kids. And she don't care a f*** about anything.'

She looked belligerent and aggressive. 'I want them done because there's something b*** wrong at the flat. Things are f*** flying all over the place.'

And so she went on. Never have I heard such a tirade of swearing, even on a construction site! I realised afterwards she didn't understand she was swearing. It was merely normal language to her and her peer group. It certainly wasn't directed against me, nor was her aggression. It was normal life and expression. After ten minutes of such rhetoric, I agreed to call and see her. With a team, of course.

'The language is a bit ripe,' I told Nicolas Hudson, one of my churchwardens.

Another member of the team was our 'learner'; someone I thought was upright and spiritually strong. Later I learned this was not so.

We arrived at the flat about 8 p.m. The grandchildren were still running around wearing only dirty tee-shirts; the three-year-old was definitely not potty trained. The flat smelled dreadful. It was an awful place.

'Sit down,' said Rosa.

We sat down tentatively, carefully avoiding obvious wet patches. She started to talk, and talk and talk... using very spicy language. I watched Nicolas' expression grow more and more incredulous. I won't attempt to repeat her dialogue – even if I could.

It appeared she had poltergeist problems. Things kept jumping off shelves and following one or other of them down the corridor. But it was all hopelessly mixed up with her very loose morals. She 'entertained' many men. Her latest 'friend' had merely offered her a lift home in his car and they had sex because 'it just happened' – even though she didn't like him very much. I gathered she had been married once, although I was confused as to the current state of that relationship.

'Do you want to bring Jesus into this situation?' I asked her. Somewhere in her past she had known about the Lord, just as she had learned about dark spiritual things as well.

'Yes, I want to get sorted out,' she replied. 'I'm b*** well fed up with my f***ing life.'

We prayed, and as I told any evil influence to 'come out in Jesus' name' so Maureen saw with spiritual eyes a 'huge black sticky ball of stuff detach itself from her, bounce across the floor, and attach itself to the learner member of the team.'

Maureen said afterwards, 'I didn't know what it meant, but I felt so uneasy.'

I too discerned at the time that all was not well, but put it down to natural feelings of revulsion. The 'learner,' whom Maureen had seen receive the 'black sticky ball,' broke away from the church. He left his wife and children and became involved in one tacky relationship after another. We discovered later that he had deliberately deceived us concerning both his spiritual commitment and his lifestyle situation.

Whenever I recall the incident, I feel a personal sense of deep sorrow and even shame. Sorrow because I lost a convert whom I thought I'd helped grow into Christian maturity; shame because I sensed I'd messed it up. Perhaps I should have seen the signs of his problem and never exposed him to such risk. Perhaps I'd wrongly ministered to Rosa when I felt in my heart that the whole situation was too complex.

Deceit is a cruel bedfellow for those seeking to minister to others. Another young man, Shane, was a stereotypical 'loser'. He was prone to whining, and over-keen to 'enjoy' sexual problems, as well as being completely tied up with his own needs. All his conversations were totally directed towards himself, and I never remember him asking any questions about the needs or concerns of others. However, he came to us one day asking for prayer. He wanted, so he said, to become a Christian. I suspected it might be merely an attention-seeking ploy, but you can never be sure. Warily I gathered a team to talk and pray with him.

'Shane, I want you to close your eyes,' Maureen spoke with authority. 'See if you can imagine a picture of Jesus, just as you think he would look.' Sanctified imagination is often an excellent way of drawing people closer to the Lord. 'Can you see him?' questioned Maureen.

'Yes, he's right there in front of me.'

'Good. Now imagine he's walking towards you...' And so the session developed, seeking to draw Shane closer to Jesus.

'What do you think Jesus would want to say to you?' I took over the leadership role, looking directly at him.

His eyes flew open and started to roll in their sockets. He moaned and was obviously agitated. Then came the spine-tingling, words: 'He's telling me that I've got to learn to be crafty.' As he spoke, a sly expression filled his face. An evil countenance was upon him and around him, and I felt chilled to the bone. A far darker entity was appearing out of Shane. And that was the one we had to deal with. However, just as we centred on the root of the need, Shane jerked up, threw his body violently round and ran out of the church.

What a disaster both these dark experiences had been! But isn't that exactly what the devil loves – to bring confusion and break-up all round? One up to Satan. At least that's how it all felt, and still feels. We should not deal lightly with the supernatural.

* * *

Our many experiences of this kind of ministry have led us to understand the depth of the spiritual darkness that lies over our patch. I'm quite certain the enemy throws out many red herrings, yet time after time God has released folk from spiritual bondage by the penetrating ministry of proclamation of the name of Jesus Christ. Our seeming failure with Shane and the learner has helped to underline that it's God's business how these things work out. The local church must train ordinary Christians to help in this kind of situation. This approach offers the possibility of excellent personal follow-up, and the very real beating back of darkness – even though there may be great personal cost. However, the risk is greater if 'helpers' seek to deceive about their personal spiritual maturity.

It is astonishing that many church leaders avoid the supernatural and seek to explain everything according to the rational understandings of this age. They fail to challenge the crafty spirits and demonic entities that hold people and areas in diabolical bondage. Such an approach allows domination by evil to prevail and tends to negate the prayer and work of Christians. Leaders who dismiss spiritual warfare as 'medieval fantasy' mislead and confuse. Christ longs to break down evil darkness, whether it be personal, or stretching in some mysterious way across a whole area. He has a myriad methods; we have merely highlighted prayer ministry.

I'm also deeply convinced of the need for continuing prayer on a daily basis to saturate areas. It seems to me that the Anglican set-up, where every person is covered by a parish church, has enormous wisdom behind it. And I look with great respect at my high church brethren who take such extreme care in public daily prayer and sacrament. They have that sense of imploring Christ to 'brood over' their area, without restricting his work to Christians. He desires all the people to be his people. Scripture says that 'God so loved *the world*,' not just Christians! (*John 3:26, italics mine*)

The local church has a pivotal place at the centre of any neighbourhood. A strong church indicates the possibility of a more godly and mature community, with a wealth of 'soul'. It is a place where the battle against the enemy is taken seriously. It is surely on God's heart to create churches that vibrantly affect their surroundings, and thereby speak into the heart of the nation. In the words of Wesley, 'And devils fear and fly...'

23

The Joshua Strategy

*March around the city once with all the armed men... make all the people
give a loud shout.*

Joshua 6:3, 5

The burley ex-SAS paratrooper looked amazed. 'That explains it all!' he
exclaimed. 'I knew them, you see – the Quinton Mob you were just
talking about. And that's where they used to meet, around the walls of
the church, just like Mary explained. They were a rough lot.'

Sam paused for a moment as he measured my response. I nodded at
him to continue.

'Did you know there was a shotgun named after them? A gunsmith in
Birmingham used to sell the Quinton Scatter Gun. And I could never
understand why the gang broke up. It happened just at the time you said.
Everybody round here was really scared of them.... except me of course.'
He smiled in recollection of past days.

'I've never heard anything like that angel story before,' he continued.
'But I really believe it, because I saw the gang break up. For no reason at
all, or so it seemed.'

I replied to Sam, 'Not just angels in the past, but here now as well:
around the church, and around the Lord's work.'

The down-to-earth part of me chuckled. Fancy a man trained to kill
and achieve military objectives by any means possible agreeing with me
about angels. But to Sam, those angels were more real than his ex-
sergeant major at Aldershot Barracks. This was the stuff of the living
God and of all eternity.

It was yet another 'envisioning evening,' and Mary and I were recalling God's work at St B's. I was delighted with the way the new course was going. After all, hadn't the ancient Jews sat round the campfire of old and recounted the deeds of Yahweh? Hadn't our Lord himself sat on his mother's knee, listening to the age-old stories of his Father's dealings with the 'chosen people'?

But there was a major snag. We were very good at recounting the past, but what about the future? It's all very well to 'envision' people with wonderful stories of God's powerful action. But if anybody had asked, 'What is the purpose? What is the vision of St B's?' I would have merely descended into generalities. Unlike the 'chosen people' we had no Promised Land in front of us, except in the sense of eternity. Yet where would the conquest stories be if Joshua had offered no leadership and no purpose to his people? The walls of Jericho would never have fallen if he had walked around seven times blowing trumpets and shouting on his own. Imagine the people of Jericho leaning nonchalantly over the top of the walls, looking scornfully down at Joshua and saying, 'Who does he think he's kidding? Oh, I feel really scared, don't you? He's a right little twit, isn't he!'

But Joshua had a vision. The whole Hebrew nation owned it, and were prepared to carry it through. And the walls came tumbling down! Similarly, we needed a vision so that the workers on our 'building site' could understand what they were building.

The question of a clear and concise vision haunted me. We'd had a whole load of words from the Lord about the church, yet somehow they had never been composited. I put the question to Mary over the breakfast table.

'You're absolutely right,' she responded firmly. 'We've got all the facts. All we need to do is put them together, sort them out in our minds, so we can make a Vision Statement.

'Why not?' she went on. 'Look at our envisioning programme right now. It's all to do with where we've come from. But we don't know where we're going to. Do you see what I mean?'

Of course I did. It was exactly how I felt!

It would have been a simple matter to impose our thoughts for a Vision Statement on the fellowship, but I remembered the example of Joshua. Of course he was a leader, but more than that the nation was involved – they were *owning* the vision. Leadership plus involvement: that's surely the key.

I called a Praise and Prayer meeting, and explained about developing a Vision Statement.

'So what I want us to do together is to hear God for St B's. Not merely the leadership, but all of us. I want you to be part of that vision.'

I sent the people off around the church building and I called them back after about an hour.

'Come on, you lot. Let's hear what God's been saying.'

The first person reported: 'I had a picture of St B's as a lighthouse, but with a dim light. God was saying, "I will provide a new battery so the light becomes bright – if you ask me and are willing to work."'

Another told of a similar 'lighthouse' understanding: 'I believe God is saying that a lighthouse is there to show the way. He wants us to "shine the light of his kingdom" through what we are – and especially through what we do.'

Many people spoke of the need for personal and corporate holiness, and the need to create a 'kingdom base' to fulfil Christ's commission. As the 'prayer pictures' rolled in, so our Vision Statement developed.

Martin Knox summed up at the end of the meeting: 'What amazes me is how the Lord has spoken similarly right across the whole fellowship. We are of one mind in the Lord. Isn't that just how it should be?' He looked around with joy in his eyes. Perhaps he was thinking that it had all been worth it – all the hard work and living here – because God was clearly on the move.

Mary and I put together the St Boniface Vision Statement, reflecting our own thoughts but especially the concepts put forward at our Praise and Prayer meeting:

St Boniface Vision Statement

1. To bring the light of Christ to a dark area

2. To make disciples by telling people what their sins are and teaching them the fear of the Lord

3. To establish a 'kingdom base' to help fulfil the Great Commission.

All around I could see people starting to understand what we were about: catching the vision, past, present and future. I determined that the church wouldn't simply drift along Sunday after Sunday, merely maintaining its 'ways'. It had to strike out with a visionary purpose that was owned by the whole church.

However, if you have a vision you have to do something about it...

24

'I've Got to Open up the Church!'

A city on a hill cannot be hidden.

Matthew 5:14

'Mrs Brown, I'm sorry to tell you that the sight from your left eye will always be less than perfect.' The eye hospital consultant looked caring and concerned. 'You see, there isn't enough light getting through to the retina, so the image sent to your brain is dim. It's like looking through a dirty window. It could get better, or it could get worse.'

He paused before continuing, 'I have to tell you that I believe it may well have been caused by a virus accelerated by stress. It must be really hard, living where you do in that council estate. It's possible the difficulties you've been through are starting to show physically.'

Have you noticed that in some Christian circles there is a prevalent view that faith is some sort of magic wand? That God is going to smooth all our pathways and make the roses grow in our garden of life? Yet it's hardly a biblical principle. The Scriptures make it abundantly clear that God doesn't remove us from the decadence and decay of the world. A simple look at John the Baptist completely wipes out such a simplistic understanding. He was a wonderful man of God and was beheaded, even though Jesus was a mere few miles away! Being a Christian, as Mary found out in hospital that morning, can be a hard and irksome task. And it takes a toll.

However, we were to discover that God can draw good out of what seems to be personal calamity. Indeed, the whole of our church outreach to the area benefited greatly from one person's seeming misfortune. And we discovered an important aspect of 'being church' in an everyday sense.

Let me tell you the story of when Jim came to 'throw in the towel' and how, in the words of St Paul, 'in all things God works for the good of those who love him.' (*Romans 8:28*)

'I'm finished with all this church business! I mean, it's just not working, is it? Be honest! I thought the Lord was going to help me sort my life out, and get back my self-respect, and now look what's happened! If there is a God in heaven, which I doubt, he can't think much of me.'

'Whoa, hang on a second!' I responded with a blinking of the eyes and a shake of the head. 'What on earth has happened to you, Jim?'

'What's happened to me? I've got to have a triple heart bypass operation. That's what's happened to me. So it's the end of my job. I mean, put that on top of my cerebral palsy, and I'm finished. Just when things were looking up. I was sorting out my money, and my kids, and my wife – then this happens. It's just not fair!'

I responded, 'Come on in and have a coffee. Tell me all about it.'

'Not likely. I've told you, I'm finished, washed up; so what's the point in talking?' And with that, Jim slammed the door behind him and was gone.

That night I called at his house to find him shamefaced and upset.

'But Wallace, I don't understand. God's been sorting out so many things and just when it's all OK: *Pow*! And I'm on the floor again.'

Jim's wife, Marge, sat with head hanging down as he continued. 'The specialist says I've got to stop work altogether, and take it very easy. And when I'm well enough, I've got to have that heart operation. Even then the consultant didn't think I would ever be very strong again. So all my plans, Wallace, they're all up the shoot, don't you think? I'll just be sitting around, and I'm only in my early forties. Why has God allowed it to happen? That's what I want to know.'

Clearly the Lord knew from the beginning that Jim was going to have angina and major surgery. As God brought him to this crossroads of faith, Jim could choose either to run away, back to the old life, or to take hold of his situation in faith. Faith means welcoming God into any crisis and asking him to lead us forward in the best way for ourselves and the kingdom.

Jim has since had major surgery – twice. He's been 'released' from his employment, and his physical health is frail. However, in the midst of his troubles he made that dynamic faith decision to look for God's hand in his trauma, and the result is that God is using him in a totally unexpected direction...

'Wallace, I hate the doors of our church being shut. It isn't right! People walk up to the building and all they ever see is a barrier. Not just a physical one, but a spiritual one too. It seems to me, somehow, that the closed doors represent a closed access to God for the people round here. I know it doesn't make sense logically, but...' He tailed off.

I was in agreement with Jim. It disturbs me how most of our church buildings stand closed and empty all week, every week. Like a testimony to a dead and closed-off God. Anyway, God had already spoken to us about being a 'door of hope', so it seemed particularly ridiculous that our physical door should always be shut.

'But what can we do?' I questioned. 'The moment we leave it open, it'll be vandalised. And the insurance company won't pay out if we don't have proper security.'

Jim looked pleased and slightly smug. 'I believe the Lord's said I've got to open up the church – every day. I can be there, you see. Marge and others will help me. We can offer coffee and help to people who visit. Or even just let them sit down to talk or pray. It can be a meeting place for anybody. Like Sam – he told me how he gets so fed up at home; with his disability there's nothing much to do. Also, I'm thinking about unemployed people, or folk who are lonely. Then there's people who just need to talk. Do you see? The church can come alive. And I can do it!'

I studied his pleased expression. 'You know we can't offer you any salary.'

'Of course not!' he replied vehemently. 'You see, it's important to me just to do this... for God. It's what I can do.'

Jim's offer had a profound effect on me. From a straightforward point of view, it fed my ego. But something deeper and more consequential nagged at me from just beneath the surface of consciousness. What could it be?

I was swimming my standard 20 lengths at the local early-birds session when the answer started to form. 'It's about our identity as a church,' I thought, nursing my breathless body forward at the halfway stage. 'We're really busy with all our prayer, counselling and groups and organised doings. But it's very unfocused, because the only "home" we have is for a couple of hours on a Sunday. To all intents and purposes we are closed off. The doors are shut. It's dead. There's no spontaneous centre of friendship and, for that matter, no sense of being "open" to the community we're supposed to be serving.'

I showered and dried with hardly a thought to the physical process, and rushed home to share my developing reflections with Mary. 'I was thinking. Jim's offer. It's more than just filling a practical need. It's as if the building site at St B's is being given a physical focus.' I concluded: 'The church building can become the centre of our heartbeat, on weekdays as well as Sundays – of our daily life; of all our outreach.'

I walked into the church on a cold Tuesday morning some months later. The little reception and coffee area was quite crowded.

'Morning, Jack. Morning, Ruth,' I nodded at one of our committed Christian couples. They had been going through a hard time – Ruth with a cancerous growth in her stomach and Jack suffering from a hernia, together with a knee cartilage problem affecting both legs.

Ruth smiled back. 'I'm so glad our church is open this morning. Jack and I needed to get out of the house to talk and pray with our friends. And I love this church; it's so peaceful.'

Some weeks earlier, while Ruth was having her cancer operation, Jack had walked in unexpectedly, and said, 'Jim, can you pray for me about Ruth? I've been hating myself ever since the specialist diagnosed Ruth's trouble, because I didn't insist that she go to the doctor's months before. Nobody knows the guilt I've been living under.'

Ted was another member of the happy little group, talking and smiling. Terry had met him in the local pub one Sunday lunchtime after church, noticed how he was slumped over his beer, and invited him to church the following week. He turned up halfway through the service, and was collared by both Terry and Jim. The story poured out: his nervous breakdown, subsequent loss of job, loss of self-respect and near marriage breakdown. Jim invited him to Open Church, and here he was. I didn't have to get involved. Jim would ensure that Ted was cared for but not over-pressured. He would receive prayer when the time was right. Befriending evangelism, coupled with Open Church, was proving to be a dynamic combination.

I was thinking, 'This beats most of our formal outreach from St B's. It's just ordinary people caring, and talking with people about the Lord. And the church being open and available. It's great.'

However, the morning wasn't finished yet. An unknown woman walked in the front door and almost immediately threw herself dramatically to the floor. Was she emotionally distressed, mentally deranged or manifesting evil spirits? I left her in the competent care of Jim and a pastoral assistant, confident that they could bring the Lord into her situation.

Jim's initiative is having a dramatic effect on the area. The church has become a sanctuary for some in deep personal need, and a meeting place for many of our members – especially those at home or retired or without work. The physical church is alive, thanks to Jim and Marge grasping hold of their troubles and turning them to the Lord in prayer.

Their initiative has led to Wednesday Church, a special service followed by coffee for older folk.

25

Sending Out the Workers

Go out quickly into the streets and alleys of the town and bring in the poor.

Luke 14:21

Even when Nancy played around the dirty streets of her back-to-back Birmingham home in the 1920s, she knew that God was God; and she loved Jesus. Perhaps it was a gift of grace, carefully fostered by her mother. However, for Nancy and her family, the church was another world; cold, formal and out of touch, it seemed to reflect everything that Jesus was not.

'Wallace, I just didn't feel welcome when I went to church. I was an outsider and nobody used to bother with me,' she reflected as I asked about her 'story'. 'So I didn't bother. It didn't seem worth it. I just prayed my own prayers at home. Anyway, I knew the Lord, so why go to a stuck-up church? The Lord isn't like that. He's warm and lovely.'

Nancy continued her story. 'Anyway, some years ago, it was soon after Christmas actually, I just felt I had to go along to church.' Her eyes lit up as she said gently, 'That's when I came to St B's. The first thing I noticed was the heaters were on and the church was actually warm. I even had to take my coat off. And it wasn't just warm physically, there was another sort of warmth as well. And after the service, I noticed everyone shared coffee and chatted together. They just made me feel part of it all. They were interested in me.'

Nancy's story is important. It highlights a simple fact we so often forget: it is vital that we truly care for people. Nancy has a sense of God. Inside. Even from her early years. But the church, not Jesus, had alienated her. Then one day she was welcomed. How important that word 'welcomed' is.

I also discovered what Nancy really meant about being welcomed. The smile and the handshake can be very cheap, and they don't always truly reflect a caring heart. They can be patronising rather than helpful. She told me, 'I felt important when Maureen came to see me. She opened up her Bible and started to read and talk about Jesus. Then she prayed for my mother who was ill and housebound. And she came back and did it again. And again. And that's when I knew people cared, about me as a person.'

Brilliant, isn't it? And so simple and straightforward. Oh, how we complicate the things of God and especially the whole idea of mission! And how we wrongly rely on the vicar or pastor to be the carer.

* * *

Nicolas Hudson is now a member of my Ministry Support Team. He, like Nancy, grew up with a sense of God in his life. He told me, 'I went to Sunday school regularly – even won prizes for my attendance. I took exams in Scripture, gaining first-class certificates. I became a Sunday school teacher and I sang in the choir. One day a lady called Grace asked me why I went to church. I told her that it was habit. Soon after, I stopped going.'

Nicolas turned up at my Vicarage some years later, wanting baptism for his daughter. As we talked, the Spirit inspired me to confront him.

'Nicolas? How would you feel about a man who said he was a footballer, but hadn't been on a football pitch for years? You would say he was living on past memories or in cloud cuckoo land, wouldn't you?'

I paused for effect before delivering the confrontational punch: 'And here's you, telling me you're a Christian, but when was the last time you were in the Lord's house?'

It always strikes me as completely amazing that from time to time God gives insight into the way people tick. I remember after Nicolas left the church office that morning I felt like a prize idiot. How dare I speak that way to somebody I'd never met before? What would he think of a vicar who gave him a lecture rather than met his felt need? I know I've occasionally spoken strongly to others, and it's the last I've seen of them. Yet with Nicolas the approach turned out to be just right. He came from a strong Christian background, but had never taken hold of faith for himself, relying instead on the faith of his parents. In his case the confrontation proved to be a catalyst, as he quietly considered his life and faith. I have since discovered Nicolas to be like Jesus' disciple Nathaniel: 'Here is a true [man], in whom there is nothing false.' (*John 1:47*) He is a man of profound integrity and thoughtful care: the sort of person any leader would be pleased to have as a right-hand man.

Nicolas' carefully considered response was to arrive at church the following Sunday. With him was baby Rosie and his 'anti-religion' wife Kate.

He writes of the experience: 'It can't have been that the church was full – there were barely 50 people in a building that could seat well over 200. Was there something about the people? The way they worshipped? The way they greeted me after the service? One young lady came and spoke to me like an old friend, and not as someone she had never seen before. Or was it that the Lord was in the place and I did not know it? As time has gone on I've realised it is indeed the Spirit of God in power. So there have been times when all I can do is fall on my knees and sob, "God, have pity on me, for I am a sinner."'

Nicolas again teaches us some basic facts. He had a 'God-awareness' in his soul. Many people have. But his sense of God had become dry and cold. He simply needed encouragement and welcoming. And the Spirit of God has done all the hard work: he has quickened his faith; he has filled Nicolas with his holy presence. Kate has also found her Saviour. Not through dramatic evangelistic pressure, but simply by being welcomed, and then meeting with the Lord in the midst of God's people. She later became our children's church leader.

There is a beautiful simplicity here. Outreach starts from 'being church'. *Being* a welcoming group. *Being* a place where the Spirit of Jesus reigns. *Being* aware that people have a God-shaped hole in them, even if they're not aware of it themselves. *Being* a place of commitment and care. *Being* a safe place where people won't talk about you behind your back. And, finally, *being* a place that shouts, 'You are needed here.' Often our outreach is ruined by our churches!

Consider for a moment whether *your* church is a place of 'being'? After all, the greatest evangelisation strategies in the world will come to nothing if there is merely a cold void awaiting seekers. The church can sometimes be the enemy of God's tactic for mission.

✳ ✳ ✳

'It isn't enough to stay within the four walls of our "safe" church building,' stated Robert Stand with a finality that boded no argument. 'Open Church is wonderful, and it's good how folk feel welcomed in the services, but Jesus didn't stay in the temple or synagogue waiting for people to come to him. Look at his preaching: on the hillsides, out of boats, around the temple walls, in ordinary people's houses, or just along the roadside. Everywhere really. And what did he say? "Go, then, to all people everywhere," (*Matthew 28:19, GNB*) and, "Go out quickly into the streets and alleys of the town and bring in the poor."' (*Luke 14:21*) So what are we going to do about it?'

'But look at what we're already doing,' I started to object. 'Guest Services, Bring-a-friend, Bereavement Services, Re-Light the candle for dedication and baptism parents, our Teddies club, holiday clubs, school assemblies...' I had to pause for a minute. 'And then there's all our special evangelistic services like Christmas and Harvest.'

I knew I was being defensive. There is a need inside most leaders to be 'see-ably successful'; to be acclaimed, even if it's mere self-acclamation. Perhaps it arises from the problem that all measurement of achievement is subjective, unless we embark on the numbers game. How can you measure pastoral support? How can you measure growth in spirituality? How can you measure the effectiveness of sermons?

I suffer from feeling like a failure, so I project success. Consequently, anyone who comes along and destroys my self-built myth is an enemy! And if my performance cannot be truly measured, how can I be accountable? Even to myself! So feelings run rampant and defence mechanisms snap into place at the slightest provocation. Speaking to colleagues, I've discovered that my feelings are fairly universal. Especially if the ministry has not even reached the simple level of an internal church support team. Some ministers look to social ministries as a way of measuring tangible achievement. I question whether extra-curriculum work is valid until a solid spiritual base has been set up locally inside the church, even though such work may feed a minister's ego.

'Wallace, hang on a minute,' said Janet frustratedly. 'You're really missing the point. Robert's not putting down what's been happening. It's great in many ways. It's just that we have to go out… And I was thinking, why not divide the parish between all our Responsibility Groups? Give them specific target-areas for evangelism? How many people live in our area?'

'About 12,000,' I obediently replied with slighted tone.

'Now, we have seven Responsibility Groups, don't we?' She stopped for a moment, as she totted up the figures. No problem to Janet, as maths had been her degree subject. 'So how about giving community zones of 1,714 to each group? Then they can pray and think and lead mission into their bit of the community.'

Janet stopped short because she saw that everyone was looking admiringly at her. Her husband gave her a hug. 'That's just right, love. It's from the Lord, I'm sure.'

* * *

Jim and Marge were out with their Responsibility Group, 'prayer-walking' their patch. Jim pointed out the garage where some years ago four children had had a horrific experience with a ouija board. They stopped and prayed.

Next they stopped at the street corner where gangs of young people loved to gather: 'Lord Jesus, come into the lives of these kids and break the hold of the dark forces that seek to keep them in bondage…' They walked on in companionable silence, seeking God's presence, when suddenly a distraught man rushed out of his maisonette. He obviously didn't know which way to turn until he saw Jim, recognising him from the church. Duncan was an occasional visitor, together with his partner.

'Jim, thank God you're here. Adele's gone and left me. She's taken the cat, left a note and gone. Right this moment. What am I going to do?'

The group stood under the street light, talking earnestly with Duncan.

'In this church, we call a spade a spade,' said Jim. 'And you've really messed up, haven't you? I mean, knocking her about and not giving her any money. It's not right, is it? So if you want us to call upon the Lord, you're going to have to repent. Tell God what your sin is. Then he can start to sort it all out. And look, you two are living together and you're not even married. So come on, get it all out in the open with the Lord.'

Instead of running after Adele, threatening violence, Duncan stood before God in the cold night air outside his house, praying for forgiveness and restoration.

The next morning, to Duncan's surprise and joy, Adele returned. What a 'coincidence' the prayer-walkers were passing at that exact moment. 'More than a coincidence,' said Jim. 'It's a God-incidence. It's God's work in response to our prayers.'

That moment led to some deep Christian counselling, and eventually the couple were married in church. The family are still together today, but sadly we never see them at St B's.

Another Responsibility Group prayerfully posted church pamphlets. They stopped in the foyer of a block of flats notorious for its disgusting state. There was excrement smeared all over the walls of the lobby, rubbish sacks split open and lying carelessly around, a window smashed and swinging as a thread of lace curtain flapped, the floor was coated with broken glass and sheer dirt. It was awful.

'I just want to pray here. To stand and bring the love of Jesus to those who live here,' said one lady with tears welling in her eyes. 'It's not right that people should live like this, even if for some it is their own fault. Anyway, my Jesus is for sinners. He would have been here, in this lobby, don't you think?'

The group prayed and still prays. Some problems are ongoing and need continual, persevering prayer – that's what prayer commitment means.

Another group conducted a service in the local old folks home. Most of the 30 or so occupants couldn't understand a word of what was being said, yet they were happy to see friends and hear the music. Dementia is a terrible thing. But Joe listened and joined in.

Martin Knox told me later that Joe was to be thrown out of the home for bad behaviour. 'It's as if he's a naughty schoolboy about to be expelled. It's crazy. I'm going to see what I can do.'

He brought Joe to church week after week, even though he would often sleep through the sermon. In fact the fellowship grew to enjoy his often loud snores. 'God's telling you something, don't you think, Wallace?' they would joke. At least I hoped they were joking.

Little by little Joe was restored. He reacted to love; he grew into a basic spirituality, and even the home began to rejoice that he was one of their 'guests'. Sometime later, at his death, the funeral in church was a touchingly poignant moment, as many church members stood quietly to remember him and affirm his eternal presence with the Lord. I suspect that without the Lord's intervention, Joe's funeral would have been one of those terrible affairs I have to conduct from time to time with only the funeral director as the solitary 'mourner'.

Weeks later, as Christmas drew near, we all stood together on a cold, windy shopping precinct. There was no one much about, and those who were just rushed by, so they wouldn't get 'caught'. However, our real-fire torches burned brightly; the helium balloons soared up into the dark sky as children 'accidentally' released them; the mince pies tasted so good. But above all, Jesus was being proclaimed. And whether or not anyone else was listening, the spiritual forces certainly were! I felt so good and happy and right. For a precious moment my heart melted and I felt I could lift up the people as a true fruit of my labour. Perhaps this was the moment of objective measurability in my ministry. Could I say with St Paul, 'Are you not the result of my work in the Lord?' (1 Corinthians 9:1)

The workers were going out into the streets and alleys of the town, beyond the four walls of the building. This was mission – reaching out from the grassroots of St B's.

26

The Lord Your God is With You

For the Lord your God will be with you wherever you go.

Joshua 1:9

It all seemed to happen with the dreamlike inevitability of a slow-motion playback. Why was it *those* six churches? Why was it *six* churches? Did all the vicars really give their approval with such ease? Did 24 people from St B's really accept the concept of being mission leaders so easily? Yet at the end of a single week it was all set up. Six Mission Partnership teams to six Anglican parishes for the six weeks of Lent.

As a congregation, we had been in danger of becoming quite insular. It was true that most folk were developing a passion to serve the neighbourhood. However, there was little understanding of the wider church, and our new, previously unchurched Christians identified only with 'our ways'. The first phase of this turning outwards, we felt, could well be towards our peer group in other Anglican churches on the estates. This would also reflect the growing burden Mary and I had for the plight of most estate churches, and underpin the emerging ministry of the whole congregation.

At the same time, we began to link with other denominations through the embryonic 'Together for Birmingham' with its clear mission statement:

> The church in [Birmingham] is made up of many congregations but in God's sight it is only one church... and... every person in

the Birmingham area must be given the opportunity to hear, experience and be persuaded of the good news in a way that they can understand.' (*Together for Birmingham*, *compiled by an ecumenical steering group under the leadership of Nick Cuthbert, leader of Riverside Church, Birmingham, 1995.*)

It was such a brilliantly straightforward concept: leaders and church congregations from across the spectrum of evangelical churches meeting for unity and mission, portraying togetherness of spirit within diversity of style. My soul yearns for such a radical togetherness of spirit which can eventually win a city for Christ. The biblical picture of Christ weeping over Jerusalem (*Luke 19:41*) is such a compelling expression of God's love. It is surely time for Christians to unify and cry over our cities. 'Together for Birmingham' passionately seeks to express its purposes through relationship, prayer, networking and events, so here was another opportunity for St B's to develop its missionary character, while at the same time focusing our Mission Partnership scheme towards other Anglican churches in similar cultural situations.

'Mission' has become a difficult concept for many outer estate churches. It summons up pictures of enabled groups of enthusiasts descending on the parish with a 'system' of evangelism and a leading speaker of dynamic ability. Small congregations worry about being invaded, and are haunted by potential failure because they have no fringe group to feed to the missioners. Financial implications are beyond thinking about, and besides missions have never worked in the past! Disappointment lurks.

Our Mission Partnership held a completely different promise. We offered a relatively small number of 'local' folk, who knew and understood council estate culture, to come and serve the church, not through grandiose schemes, but with a listening ear. Indeed, for each Mission Partnership, the first job of the core group of four people was simply to go and listen prayerfully to the minister and other leaders, then gradually and quietly develop a gentle plan which could be initiated and owned by the congregation. This would enable them to accept and appreciate that God really did care about their church and had his specific and unique way forward for them. At the same time, it was made quite clear that partnership was of great benefit to us. It offered the possibility of overviewing other churches' needs and then sharing our faith in a non-threatening environment. What a privilege and opportunity! All in all, we were likely to be net gainers from the experience.

The Mission Partnerships had all been agreed over the phone, most with vicars I hardly knew. Then, just a few days later, I took Jim and Marge to an estate church in south Birmingham to introduce them as leaders of the next Mission Partnership team. Jim and Marge emerged an hour later from their meeting with the vicar, both beaming.

'It went great. All we did was ask him about his parish, and what he thought was needed. I think he was quite surprised because he expected us to come and present some sort of "package deal" which he'd have to agree to. He didn't expect us just to sit and listen, and then pray, and then listen to God.'

Marge enthused: 'And Wallace, the Lord really spoke to us all. It was obvious that he was there.'

They went on to tell me about the church. 'It's only a small fellowship, of about 20 folk. And most of them seem really set in their ways. The vicar said they wanted new people, especially young families. But whenever anyone comes along, they sort of close ranks. It's like a clique that doesn't want to be a clique but is a clique.' She shook her head and smiled. 'Do you understand? Anyway, we're all meeting for prayer next week.'

Jim said, 'So it's all started, you see!'

'It hasn't just started,' Mary commented later that evening. I was in the midst of lighting our coal fire in the newly arranged vicarage hearth.

'Humph,' I replied, thinking she was talking about my near abortive efforts at fire-raising. 'It's this smokeless coal stuff that's the problem.'

She furrowed her brow. 'What's that, you say?' Amazing how two people can talk about different things at the same time. 'Oh I see, the fire. Well I was talking about the Mission Partnerships. They haven't just started because it actually began almost exactly three years ago today.'

I noticed for the first time her 'famous' prophecy book open on her lap. 'Here it is, word for word: "I had a picture of St B's with God's hand of blessing over it. As he lifted his hand, light shot out to various places. God was saying that what he is giving us now is to share with others. We must go where he sends us."'

Her eyes lit up as she continued, 'And somebody else had this picture: "Wallace is organising groups to go out. God wants us to be a church with an open door and yet with an open roof, so that people can be released out for God's work."'

'Do you see?' she enthused. 'Our Mission Partnerships may just be starting. But in reality they began years ago. God certainly knows what he is doing!'

* * *

'I commission you, in the name of the Father, the Son and the Holy Spirit,' proclaimed the Archdeacon of Birmingham as he moved among the twelve or so members of the first Mission Partnership team and laid hands upon each and every one. 'Go to the parish of... Jesus said, "Go and make disciples and teach them to obey everything I have commanded... I will be with you always, to the very end of the age."'

The next team came forward, then the next, right through the six teams. Alongside and with great gusto and excitement, children waved the specially made banners representing all the Mission Partnership churches. After all, they were equally part of it. The church was full and overflowing. It was a wonderful moment; the climax of many years of pain and toil and seeming adversity. Later in his talk, the Archdeacon mentioned the biblical sending out of the 70 disciples, and I suddenly realised it was the very figure going out. Brilliant!

The Mission Partnerships themselves turned out to be both lovely and painful. Jim summed up one of the joys as he recounted his experience as a Mission Core Group leader: 'The highlight for me was helping them to cope with the aftermath of a local murder. Because Marge and I had personally experienced a murder situation just a few doors away from our own home, we could totally empathise with them. So we suggested a small group of us went out to pray on location for God's love and peace to overcome the sense of violence and terror. We had an amazing time of togetherness in the Lord and breaking down the powers of darkness. Whoever would have thought that mission meant praying over a murder scene!'

On the other hand, one of the churches has since closed down. Despite our constant prayers, and even some of our missioners joining them for a long and painful period of several years, the congregation just wilted away. How often the Christian life leaves one with a feeling of helplessness, even in the midst of knowing that our God is sovereign and all powerful. The reality of Jesus Christ, the mighty Son of the living God, hanging on the cross of Calvary, depicts this so poignantly.

The ministry of Mission Partnership continued to develop in an unexpected direction. Over the year 2000, a roadshow organised by the Church Pastoral Aid Society gave Mary and me the opportunity to teach leaders of all denominations about servant ministry to the estates of towns and cities all over the UK. At each roadshow location, four different members of our congregation shared the joys and pain of being part of a Christian community within the estate environment. These testimonies from ordinary Christians, who live everyday life among the new poor of our society, moved even hardened ministers to tears.

God's calling grows seemingly every year, not just to work alongside evangelicals, but right across the spectrum of church styles. Indeed, it was through a 'picture' I received during a service at the monastic community of Taizé in France that God revealed the sheer breadth of his calling to us. I had been really concerned about relationships with church leaders who did not share my evangelical understandings; theologically, it was as though we were on a different planet. Should I really be longing for their churches to grow? Then God spoke as I listened to the wonderful surging back and forth of a Taizé chant. I saw myself in a darkened room. The venetian blind was down to block the light, although it was somehow clear that the sun was shining brightly outside. And then it was as if God himself tweaked the blind control to show first a little and then a greater amount of light while saying, 'Wallace, don't worry about your understanding or the amount of light that's not there. Rejoice in the light that is there.' I knew then that I was to be really delighted to work fully with all manner of church styles: to applaud the light I perceived. My business was not to judge, but to speak of his angels and his power and his love in the context of the 'hidden poor'. It's wonderful to work in partnership with God, but I have to realise time and time again just who the Senior Partner is!

For us at St B's, that time of developing Mission Partnerships was in many ways the pinnacle of ministry, and somehow demonstrated God's loving concern for us as a very ordinary estate congregation. It epitomised the extent of the journey we had travelled: from the 'angels on the walls' revelation in the context of our depressed and run-down parish church, to becoming a lively fellowship sending 70 of its members on Mission Partnerships to six churches throughout Birmingham. Yet even today, when one expects to be in the comfort zone of a full, thriving church, God is still moving us on. At the time of writing, the church has just sent out about a third of the congregation to plant a sister congregation in the midst of one of the estates. Life is never comfortable for a church that is seeking to listen to God!

And, as I always think when I'm reminded that God is the Senior Partner: this is just the beginning.

27

Conclusion

In the twenty-first century, many council estates are clearly in a state of crisis. A report from the Joseph Rowntree Foundation tells us:

> 12 of the 13 [riots and violent disturbances of 1991/2] took place in council estates, most of which were large. All were low-income areas with long-standing social problems. All bar one comprised largely traditional houses with gardens. (*Anne Power and Rebecca Tunstall, Joseph Rowntree Foundation.*)

Why should it be so? The reasons are manifold and complex, but arise out of the striking sociological and spiritual changes of the last few generations.

The accepted 'working-class' flavour of the outer estates has changed radically to a 'benefit-dependent culture' (*Wallace and Mary Brown, 'The Hidden Poor, 1996*); the traditional Christian moral background has been plundered by postmodernism; one-parent families abound; on many estates gangs loiter on street corners, domestic violence escalates, drink dominates, children swear at passers-by, and drugs are readily available.

By and large, the flats, maisonettes and houses of these large estates were erected on greenfield sites during the four post-war decades. The concept of rehousing families from the demolished slums, as well as housing the growing population, was good. Indeed, in the 1950s the planners' 'grand vision' was summed up by the words of the then Bishop of Birmingham: 'New estates, well designed and spacious, are being swiftly built.' (*Bishop John Leonard Wilson, 'Circles without Centres', Birmingham Diocesan Report, 1951*). And certainly much of the housing was of fair quality, albeit squeezed together. On the other hand, there were many hastily erected tower blocks, only fit for demolition. Furthermore, even today I meet and sympathise with families whose lives are focused around concrete prefabricated damp traps, where one can hear the neighbours use the toilet! In the year 2000, somewhere between a third and half of all Birmingham people live in such local authority built accommodation. It is on these estates that we meet the huge populace of the 'hidden poor' of our British society.

Generally speaking, our estates were built for the working man and his family who, in days gone by, were seen to embody the 'salt of the earth', working-class ethic. And although church attendance was far from strong (*Bishop David Sheppard showed that less than one person in a hundred of 'working class' parishes were on the Electoral Roll of their local church. He later qualifies 'working class' as 'consisting mainly of council housing'. Built as a City, Hodder & Stoughton, 1974*), there was an overall sense of adherence to traditional values and virtues. It is remarkable that as social norms have deteriorated, so church attendance has fallen by more than 50 per cent! On today's estates, a mere four adults per thousand population attend an Anglican church on any given Sunday. And out of an overall population approaching a quarter of a million people, fewer than 300 children (aged 0-16 years) enter through the (occasionally) open doors!

Not only are estates in crisis; so also are estate churches.

And there is certainly a profound link between the two situations. From detailed observations of the past 14 years, I have concluded that the church has lost touch with the estates, and the estates have lost touch with their church. So what can be done? Whatever the answer, it certainly has to start with the church reaching out to, and connecting with, the people of the outer estates. This, at the very least, means a radical reform of how we perceive and go about our Christian mission to 'Go and make disciples'. (*Matthew 28:19*)

I remember reading of a prophetic insight that was to become the radical basis of Mike Bickle's developing ministry (Mike was Pastor to the colourful, not to say controversial, Kansas City Prophets.) God said to him, 'I will change the understanding and expression of Christianity in the earth.' (*Mike Bickle, Growing in the Prophetic, Kingsway 1995*) Mike Bickle goes on to say, 'The phrase "the understanding of Christianity" means the way Christianity is perceived by unbelievers.'

On the estates, the Christian church is perceived as irrelevant. It is for older 'religious' women, a sort of stuffy club that 'tut-tuts' at the modern lifestyle. People often think that it is state-funded and merely a ready facility for christenings, weddings and funerals – a sort of social 'right' organised by the vicar. Furthermore, few mothers (and even fewer fathers) bother with christening these days, where marriage is out of date and/or financial suicide for those on benefit. So the church (and perhaps God) fades more and more into the background.

It is a terrible truth that as the church continues to lose touch with the society it seeks to serve, this perception of irrelevance escalates. Furthermore, and quite unforgivably, it has lost its vibrant, exciting faith and the resulting ability to connect the people of the neighbourhood with the living God. Instead it wallows in the midst of the dire social needs of the 'hidden poor' rather than being a prophetic signpost. The outer-estate churches themselves are, in the main, part of the problem rather than part of the answer. Rescue for the 'hidden poor' starts with the spiritual rescue of the church, so that God's heart of salt and light can be injected into the community.

Do not be deceived into thinking that people on the estates are no longer spiritual. Far from it. In our postmodern society there is a profound searching for spirituality, but because of the seeming lack of relevance, few people look to the church of the living God. The church accidentally interfaces with this false perception: I have discovered that most estate churches package the 'God product' in such a way as to alienate many and most ordinary people.

Take St Anybody's Church. It meets every Sunday in a concrete 60s-style building in the middle of the estate. The building itself appears quite well kept-up in a rather dated fashion, but as you get nearer, the senses are invaded by high tri-pointed fencing, rolled razor wire fortifying the flat roof, a crudely graffitied notice board bravely declaring a long past rummage sale, and an atmosphere of lonely dereliction.

Inside, the vague smell of lavender polish competes with the musty odour of suffocated air. The chairs are fixed in place and you just know from the very atmosphere that you have to be most careful where (and when) you sit.

On the surface the people are not particularly friendly. However, you feel they really want to welcome you, but are somehow rather shy and don't quite know what to say. They hand you a couple of books and a dog-eared piece of paper, with a sort of nervous half-smile.

The service starts as the vicar enters and the small group of mostly elderly ladies rises to its feet. Without so much as a 'good morning' the first hymn crashes out. It's played by a stalwart lady with a determined expression. The musical pitch is too high, so the valiant attempts at the soaring notes assault the ear. One of the ladies obviously greatly values herself as a soprano and her voice rises, shrill, above the others.

The hymn ponders on: your bored eyes stray over the page and you even begin to note the dates of the composer's birth and death. Some mental arithmetic leads to a working out of their age when they died. This reverie evolves into a lethargic ruminating as to who was king, or was it queen, in 1649? Or was it Cromwell?

'Please be seated.' The sermon starts. You note with initial interest that the preacher speaks with great clarity. However, the content does not seem terribly attention-grabbing, so again your concentration wanders. How many bricks are there in the back wall? You look at the hat of the lady in front. You notice that the speaker has cleared his throat – again. The lady at the organ is fiddling with her music, and you wonder what's going on in her mind. Whoops, you're supposed to be thinking about God!

At the end of the hour, somebody bravely offers you a coffee. But somehow there is that feeling of intruding into the Silver Threads club. A quick exit seems a good idea, with an internal thought: 'Thank goodness I didn't bring the kids.'

Of course this description is a total stereotype, but my personal experience leads me to the conclusion that it's often not so far from the mark. I'm forced to the basic question: 'Why should this be so?' Again and again I come back to my informed perception: outer-estate churches dominated by small power groups of established 'respectable' bulwarks of 50s lifestyle and breeding are perceiving their role to be retainers of church 'as it should be', as it was in their generation, where they feel comfortable and in control. 'Of course we welcome children,' they would say. But always on their terms of 'seen and not heard'. Tell that to a millennium child! There is an inner hope of restoration, but experience tells them it's fairly hopeless and they feel a keen sense of failure, so it's better not to talk about it. Of course, any able, dynamic leaders have long since departed the estate, having bought their own houses and settled into a 'nice' neighbourhood. The remnant struggle on. Determined to keep things going, but without hope or plan. One day the golden era will return... maybe!

Such churches fail to understand they are operating within a completely changed context of society. Today's society is postmodern. Consequently many and most of our present-day estate churches are reaching out with the gnarled, aged arms of the post-war culture into a society that venerates the new, the young and the self. Little wonder they are dying on their feet!

St Anybody's Church is existing in a historic time warp and offers no answers for the millennial generation. In fact it hasn't even sorted out the questions! Consequently it is dying. Yet that is not the way of the Spirit of God: he continually raises prophetic signposts for each generation. The Father guides his people to speak meaningfully to every culture. Of course the message of the gospel does not change, but it must be expressed to give understanding within cultural 'receiving zones'. As the writer of the letter to Hebrews says, 'Jesus Christ is the same yesterday and today and for ever.' (*Hebrews 13:8*) It's merely the presentation that has to alter.

The purpose of this book

Angels on the Walls seeks to break the mould of council-estate 'religion'. Not by paying homage to the new culture, but by re-presenting the eternal truths of God so they can be understood and acted upon by the present and rising generation. Over the past years, St Boniface Church has built up an all-age and truly local Christian community which has clearly become salt, yeast and light within the three estates it serves. The whole neighbourhood has been given a new hope and possibility for the future.

The precepts of *Angels on the Walls* outlined above are not limited to council estates. It is true that Bishops Roger Sainsbury and Laurie Green, on behalf of the Urban Bishops Panel in a letter to the *Church of England Newspaper*, rightly spoke about estates being 'the coal-face… of mission and ministry' (*Church of England Newspaper, 21st November 1997*), but postmodernism is a fact right across our third-millennium society. What is happening on the estates today will happen across the broader face of society tomorrow. Either the church of God gets stuck into its 'coal-face', whatever and wherever that may be, or it will suffer the redundancy of irrelevance.

The angels have made their choice.

Appendix

Clipboard

This appendix highlights principles of ministry offered in the book. Strategies can and should be adopted by individual ministers and churches, but those strategies must arise from foundational principles, because principles seek to establish basic truth.

1. Hear God

Moses himself rediscovered and developed this 'ministry principle'. As he led the Hebrews towards the Promised Land, he was continually challenged to bring all the nearly disastrous situations back to God. 'God, show me again what I should do,' was his plain cry.

Today's church must learn to discern God's prophetic voice through the word and the Spirit, and then act accordingly.

- Listen to God, hear what he says and obey his word. (Chapter 1)
- Use 'God ideas' rather than 'good ideas'. (Chapter 1)
- Seek God's plan through the prophetic, rather than short-term pragmatic solutions. His way leads to his answer! (Chapter 4)
- Pray and fast... it was good enough for Jesus! (Matthew 4:2)
- Remember: God is always bigger than any human situation.

2. Establish a firm spiritual base

There is no future in seeking to move any congregation on to new things until a firm spiritual base has been established. Such a pathway calls for a straightforward proclamation of the gospel as well as a continual experience of the presence of God the Holy Spirit. It can often be a distressing and even traumatic pathway as the people, who are the church, re-establish their confidence/commitment in Christ. (Chapter 5)

Individually

- Lack of sin-awareness is a major issue in postmodern Britain. Society has turned its back on God and ignores his eternal reality and truth. (Chapter 14)
- Original and active sin are present-day realities. They darken everyone's soul. Teach repentance and faith. (Chapter 14)
- Jesus said we must 'make disciples' rather than 'converts'. Commitment, growth, prayer ministry and wholeness through Christ must be developed. (Matthew 28:19)
- People need support to grow. Wild grapes need long-term cultivation. (Chapter 15)
- Help the helped to become the helpers. God can be welcomed into the midst of any crisis. (Chapter 19)

Corporately

- Develop all-member ministry and all-member responsibility.
- Tackle slavery to any ecclesiastical system. (Chapter 8)
- Don't allow church to become a 'nostalgic haven'. (Chapter 5)
- Teams rather than omnicompetent ministers are God's way of working. Select the team through prayer and calling rather than expediency. (Chapter 10)
- Leading services should be corporate. (Chapter 9)
- Keep telling the faith story of how God has been at work in your church. (Chapter 23)
- Help the congregation to develop and own God's vision for the church's future. (Chapter 23)

- Be aware that young people and children are spiritual beings – they are part of today's church and not mere appendages. Sunday school / youth club models must be faith building. (Chapter 17)
- Remember: The church and leadership are under God's authority.

3. Engage in spiritual warfare

On many estates, godlessness reigns. This godlessness has often led to dark spiritual forces dominating certain areas with a consequent escalation in lawlessness. A doorway has been opened.

The estate church will see no major growth until such forces are dealt with on a spiritual plane. The spiritual affects the physical. However, this spiritual battle doesn't end with the first, second or hundredth prayer (Ephesians 6:12). It surges back and forth as in a battlefield. But the victory is already assured by Jesus.

The people of God must rise up from being victims to become conquerors – in Christ's name!

- Accept the truth of God's word about the supernatural. (Ephesians 6:12)
- Recognise that we are involved in an ongoing spiritual battle with the powers of darkness. (Chapter 18)
- The spiritual profoundly affects the physical. (Chapter 4)
- We are co-workers with the Holy Spirit. Link spirituality with hard work! (Chapter 6)
- God can and does instigate neighbourhood regeneration through the faith community. (Chapter 18)
- Pray on location wherever possible. Some sort of 'spiritual mapping' is essential for this to be an effective tool. (Chapter 18)
- God-incidences happen when we grasp spiritual realities. (Chapter 18)
- Remember: The deepening spiritual awareness of a small group can (and does) affect the whole church community

and dynamically shines the light of Christ into the neighbourhood.

4. Incarnational ministry

'Enabled' Christians moving into the heart of council estates can make a life or death difference to the local church. Most other caring agencies operate through professional people who live at a distance and hold themselves separate from the dynamics of everyday estate living.

The Christian gospel is all about the God who 'made himself nothing, taking the very nature of a servant, being made in human likeness' (Philippians 2:7). Likewise, and in the example of our Lord, there are terrific missionary opportunities on the estates of the third millennium.

Often, such 'missionaries' can help form a potent support team with the usually lonely, often isolated and sometimes desperate local minister.

- Sacrificial, incarnational ministry is God's way in Christ. (Chapter 9)
- Missionaries are needed. God longs to 'bring in' enabled church workers. They can be 'spiritual scaffolding' as well as start the process of 'the helped becoming the helpers'. (Chapter 10)
- Incarnational ministry is intensely costly at a personal level – expect physical, emotional and spiritual exhaustion. (Chapter 13)
- Incarnational missionaries can often form the basis for a Ministry Support Team. (Chapter 9)
- 'Incarnational' support by enabled Christians helps poor churches. (Chapter 9)
- Faith risks encourage profound spiritual growth within the 'missionary'. (Chapter 13)

5. Address cultural issues

Estate churches must be *in* the local culture, but not *of* the local culture. Estate churches must be at the cutting edge of a radical rethink of 'being church', so welcoming the local community. At the same time we must maintain our definitiveness as a Christian community, so people can see that we are what we are.

- Most estates comprise fractured neighbourhoods rather than significant communities. The dire needs of such areas are often hidden, even from the people who live there! Churches can offer a pivotal role in understanding and developing the local community. (Chapter 19)
- Sociologically, estates have changed beyond all recognition in the last few generations. The working-class ethic has all but gone. Respond to the shifting trend towards a postmodern, benefit-dependent culture. (Chapter 19)
- Empower the disempowered. (Chapter 11)
- Decide which community group the church is seeking to serve. Develop an understanding of their culture. Reach out and connect with the community, thereby demonstrating that God's church is alive. (Chapter 24)
- Don't compromise the distinctiveness of the gospel. (Chapter 7)
- Build a church community – not just a Sunday club. (Chapter 19)
- Remember: godliness leads to lawfulness.

6. Leadership

The Anglican ordination service says:

> Because you cannot bear the weight of this ministry in your own strength but only by the grace and power of God, pray earnestly for His Holy Spirit. Pray that He will each day enlarge and enlighten your understanding of the Scriptures, so that you may grow stronger and more mature in your ministry, as you fashion your life and the lives of your people on the word of God.

Brilliant, isn't it? And not just for Anglicans. It reflects the whole power, anointing and responsibility of being a leader of the church of God. Ministers are called to be 'servant leaders' of the Christian community as well as missionaries to the whole of society itself.

- Sometimes leaders have to confront and even destroy in order to build up. Pruning hurts! (Chapter 5)
- Leaders are accountable to God for actions and decisions. (Chapter 7)
- Leaders must lead – as well as enable others. (Chapter 20)
- Leaders need friends. (Chapter 9)
- Leaders need to be vulnerable and admit they make mistakes. This allows others to 'fail'. (Chapter 10)
- Leaders are not to be omnicompetent despots. Churches need to be leader-led and not leader-dominated. (Chapter 20)
- Develop a leadership team. (Chapter 10)
- Pastoral concern must reflect truth rather than seeking always to be 'nice'. (Chapter 14)
- Offer truth even if it doesn't grow membership. (Chapter 14)
- Leaders must ensure that the fellowship accepts and owns the way forward. Teaching is of prime importance. (Chapter 18)

The End

The god of this age has blinded the minds of unbelievers, so that they cannot see the light of the gospel of the glory of Christ, who is the image of God. For we do not preach ourselves, but Jesus Christ as Lord, and ourselves as your servants for Jesus' sake. For God, who said, 'Let light shine out of darkness' made his light shine in our hearts to give us the light of the knowledge of the glory of God in the face of Christ. But we have this treasure in jars of clay to show that this all-surpassing power is from God and not from us.

2 Corinthians 4:4

Printed in Great Britain
by Amazon